BEAUTIFUL BACKYARDS

BEAUTIFUL BACKYARDS

COURTYARDS • TERRACES • PATIOS • DECKS • BALCONIES

SIMPLE IDEAS AND TECHNIQUES TO TRANSFORM YOUR
OUSIDE SPACE, WITH 280 PRACTICAL PHOTOGRAPHS

Joan Clifton and Jenny Hendy

southwater

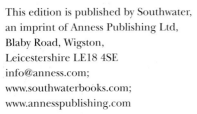

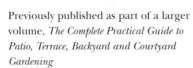

This edition is published by Southwater, an imprint of Anness Publishing Ltd, Blaby Road, Wigston, Leicestershire LE18 4SE
info@anness.com;
www.southwaterbooks.com;
www.annesspublishing.com

If you like the images in this book and would like to investigate using them for publishing, promotions or advertising, please visit our website www.practicalpictures.com for more information.

Publisher: Joanna Lorenz
Editorial Director: Helen Sudell
Project Editor: Emma Clegg
Designer: Abby Franklin
Practical photography: Howard Rice
Illustrator: Robert Highton
Production Controller: Ben Worley

© Anness Publishing Ltd 2012

Previously published as part of a larger volume, *The Complete Practical Guide to Patio, Terrace, Backyard and Courtyard Gardening*

PUBLISHER'S NOTES

Although the advice and information in this book are believed to be accurate and true at the time of going to press, neither the authors nor the publisher can accept any legal responsibility or liability for any errors or omissions that may have been made nor for any inaccuracies nor for any loss, harm or injury that comes about from following instructions or advice in this book.

Great care should be taken if you include pools, ponds or water features as part of your garden landscape. Young children should never be left unsupervised near water of any depth, and if children are able to access the garden all pools and ponds should be fenced and gated to the recommended specifications

CONTENTS

INTRODUCTION

In recent years the backyard or patio has seen a reincarnation. The small, enclosed garden is the natural result of the need to maximize our urban spaces. It also offers a sanctuary from the noise and pollution around us. The design potential of these private areas, as extensions to our homes and as places of relaxation, is strongly evident in the work of modern architects and designers.

Above: *Stone pavers such as these are a traditional style of patio flooring.*

The design that you choose for your patio will depend on many factors, from its aspect and soil quality to your own style preferences. This book sets out to unravel some of the options for a contained outside area, with design hints, useful plants, practical features and inspiring ways of making it your own.

A chapter called Planning Your Backyard explains how to assess your site, freshen up a neglected courtyard and then plan a more permanent design. The next section on Style Options focuses on six concepts for patio styles – Formal Spaces, Mediterranean Retreats, Open-air Sanctuaries, Productive Sites, Peaceful Havens and Modern Zones. Choose one of these, or draw ideas from several to define the visual approach to your own space. You might prefer orderly proportions and classical features, or perhaps a minimal, streamlined area using contemporary and experimental materials. Perhaps a calm, private paradise is more your style, a solitary refuge for moments of quiet contemplation. Alternatively, you can opt for bright colours, atmospheric scents and a comfortable area for relaxing and socializing. Indeed a patio can be designed to create an extension to your home, a real-life living space, with interior styling, and a place to cook, eat, relax,

welcome friends, bathe and sleep. A decorative kitchen garden might also be the order of the day, somewhere to cultivate fresh vegetables and fruit and flowers for the table.

A third section profiles six Case Studies of individual patios. Each one includes an illustrated garden plan, practical advice on creating elements relevant to the location and two step-by-step methods of how to create key features. The techniques are chosen in character with the case study, but many of them are interchangeable – such as laying random paving, painting a rendered wall, or lighting a pathway

– and would be useful features to integrate in any courtyard.

Plants are the reason we create a garden and to help make your choice the final section, Planting Choices, identifies suitable types of plants by their form and function, appearance, seasonality and growing requirements.

The patio is a garden in miniature. It gives you the opportunity to enact any decorative or horticultural fantasy, classical or romantic, spare or productive that you desire. So use the wealth of ideas in the chapters that follow to create a special outdoor space that extends your home.

Left: *Changes of level introduce interest to a long, narrow site. The rectilinear paving is softened by the canal and the curved wall.*

Right: *This spacious first-floor patio has an architectural emphasis with interior styling.*

PLANNING YOUR BACKYARD

The first stage when starting work on a new garden, or renovating an old one, is to assess its condition, make some plans and smarten up the framework. This chapter shows how to assess a patio's good and bad points critically and how to deal with any shortfalls imaginatively. With the knowledge collected from carrying out a site survey, you will be able to make practical building and planting decisions, and adapt the appearance and setting of the courtyard to suit your needs.

There are plenty of things you can do quickly and easily to improve a space. This chapter shows some basic techniques to smarten up a neglected patio area, as well as how to draw up paper plans for a complete design makeover. The more thorough your preparation, the easier it will be to realize your design. Plants will have the best possible start and you are then able to make your patio garden a really special place.

Left: *Bold planting, a fresh coat of paint and stylish new floor tiles have transformed this basement garden into an urban oasis.*

ASSESSING THE SITE

Before beginning work, it's important to carry out a thorough site survey. Key points to consider are the amount of sunlight various parts of the garden receive, relative degrees of shelter or exposure, the acidity or alkalinity of the soil, and drainage. If you are new to the garden and can wait a season before starting, you will be able to map out where plants are and what you would like to keep.

Above: *Aim to create a pleasing balance between hard landscaping and greenery.*

Above: *Courtyards can be sheltered from wind but may sacrifice light as a result. Use plants that will thrive in your courtyard's specific microclimate.*

Light and Aspect

In more open gardens, the points at which the sun rises in the morning (east) and sets in the evening (west) are easy to calculate through simple observation. This gives you an idea of which are the sunniest and warmest areas of the garden (south- and west-facing parts) and which are the cooler, shadier regions (north- and east-facing parts). However, in small and enclosed courtyards and on terraces, using compass points may not be helpful, since walls, buildings and large specimen plants or trees may block out the sun during the main part of the day, even if the garden faces due south.

Make a sketch of your garden and mark on it the rough distribution of light as it moves throughout the day, in particular the sunniest areas and the shadiest areas. These findings should inform your planting decisions more than any other factors.

Reducing Wind Turbulence

Wind turbulence caused by the position of surrounding buildings can be damaging to plants and structures. It can also make sitting out in the garden less than pleasant. Map where these vortices are so that you can plan natural or artificial windbreaks to reduce wind speed and create sheltered oases. Robust trees and deciduous shrubs as well as hedges make efficient wind breaks because they filter the air. Solid barriers, such as fences, can create even more turbulence. In addition to plants, try fixing windbreak mesh on to the back of trellis screens or use loose woven screens, such as wattle hurdles.

Soil Type and Drainage

Many courtyard gardens will already be paved or covered with solid concrete. Alternatively, you may want to put fresh paving down. In these cases the soil is buried and therefore its quality is of no consequence.

However, in courtyards that need soil, a healthy soil structure requires air exposure. So compacted soil without air spaces or soil that is too wet will support only a limited range of plants, earthworms and microorganisms. At the other end of the spectrum, very dry soil that drains rapidly, such as sandy or stony soil, also poses problems. Nutrients are washed from the rooting zone of plants and the lack of moisture means that only drought-tolerant types, such as succulents and hardy herbs, thrive.

Above: *Overcome a lack of planting space or poor soil by using large planters.*

ESTABLISHING YOUR SOIL TYPE

You need to know the soil characteristics of your garden so that you can choose the appropriate cultivation technique. Divided into three types – clay, sand and loam – each soil has a specific visual and handling quality.

Loam is the easiest soil to manage, but you can work on both clay and sandy soils to make them just as productive. Remember, too, that some plants actually prefer sand or clay.

Clay soil This can easily be formed into a ball shape. Your soil will be clay if water pools on the soil surface, or it sticks to your boots in winter and dries hard in summer. Clay soil is the most fertile, but can have drainage problems. To improve poorly drained clay, dig in grit and bulky organic matter, such as well-rotted manure or spent mushroom compost (soil mix).

Sandy soil This disintegrates when you try to form it. A light-coloured, free-draining soil, it is constantly thirsty in summer and is the poorest quality soil. Mulch sandy soil with manure to make it more moisture retentive and fertile. Do this by covering the surface of the damp soil with a thick mulch of well-rotted manure.

Loam or silt You can form loam into a ball that crumbles under pressure. A mixture of sand and clay, this is the best balanced soil and poses few cultivation problems. Loams are usually dark because of their high humus content (decayed organic matter), but lighter soils can be improved by digging in manure.

TESTING YOUR SOIL PH

All plants prefer soil that has a particular level of acidity or alkalinity, and this is measured on the pH scale. Therefore, soil pH is an important factor when deciding which plants will thrive in your garden. Expressed as a scale ranging between 1 and 14, 1 is highly acidic while 14 is extremely alkaline. A soil reading at 7 is neutral. Test pH meters are available at most garden centres. Some plants, such as azaleas, rhododendrons, conifers and blueberries, prefer acid soils, whereas vegetables,

grasses and most ornamentals like a slightly alkaline soil. The sequence below shows you how to measure the pH of your soil.

Having established the soil pH, depending on the plants you want to include, you can increase or, less successfully, decrease the soil pH. To make the soil less acidic (and raise the pH), apply a material containing lime, such as ground agricultural limestone or calcified seaweed. Don't try acidifying soil for rhododendrons.

1 After loosening several different areas of soil, moisten using rainwater (tap water could give false readings) and allow this to soak through the ground for a few minutes.

2 Using a trowel, take a sample of the wet soil from the first patch only and place it in a clean, dry jar, adding more rainwater if necessary ready for the reading.

3 Always clean and dry the probe on the pH meter first to eliminate the risk of an incorrect reading. It is important to do this between each soil reading.

4 Push the probe into the moist soil sample and wait a few moments until the needle stops moving. The readout will show how acidic or alkaline each sample is.

UPGRADING THE SITE

It is amazing how effective spring cleaning a site can be. Small, enclosed gardens often end up as repositories for junk, including left-over materials from home renovations. So, start by clearing out the rubbish, followed by cleaning, weeding and pruning. This is also the time to check basics, such as garden drainage, as well as the integrity of walls, fences, paving and any existing structures.

Above: *Attach a discreet support framework of wires for climbers such as clematis.*

Far left: *Consider replacing tiny lawns with easy-care planting and surfacing.*

Left: *Building raised beds with sympathetic materials creates new planting opportunities.*

Simplifying Floors and Boundaries

If your garden boundaries are made up of mismatched fencing panels or walls with different paint or trellis coverings, the space may not be showing itself to its best advantage. An inexpensive yet effective way to hide mismatched surfaces is to cover them with a roll of brushwood or bamboo screening. You can quickly attach this to existing fencing using a heavy-duty staple gun.

To simplify the garden floor, to create a feeling of space and to smarten its appearance, treat it as you would a room in the home and have the space decked, paved, tiled or covered with gravel to hide any uncoordinated surfaces.

Flooring Fixes

Unloved paving or concrete can be effectively rejuvenated using a pressure washer to remove all surface grime and algae (see also page 246). And if you can't match up broken paving slabs, try filling the gaps with bricks, setts or cobbles rather than repaving the whole area. This is also an excellent way to add texture and interest to plain paving.

Areas of concrete are often problematic, as removing thick slabs of this material is both difficult and expensive. A suggestion for camouflaging concrete is given below. Another option is to pave the concrete over with slabs – however, if the slabs are abutting a house or garage wall keep them well below the damp-proof course (usually two bricks depth). Other surfacing ideas include thin, non-slip ceramic, slate or limestone tiles, or gravel and slate chippings. You could also suspend a deck over the concrete, leaving a gap with the house wall.

CAMOUFLAGING CONCRETE

Use gravel to hide areas of concrete. There are many types and grades of gravel, from limestone chippings, peagravel (a well-rounded gravel) and hoggin (a mixture of clays, sand and gravel), to the more decorative and expensive aggregates. Loose surfaces laid over concrete may pose a slip risk, so add a solid pathway of slabs, decking tiles or stepping-stones.

1 Lay your gravel to a depth that is thick enough so that the concrete does not show through when the gravel is walked on.

2 Rake the gravel over until it is level. You may need to do this regularly depending on the foot traffic it receives.

RENOVATING PAINTED WALLS

Painted walls start to look neglected after a few years and so need repainting from time to time. As structural elements of the courtyard, renovated walls provide you with a canvas on which to apply various design ideas.

Before repainting a wall, first carry out all necessary repairs and surface preparations, including repointing any brickwork where the mortar is crumbling or replastering any damaged areas of rendering. Be aware that algal growth on walls, which can show up prominently on whitewashed surfaces, is not only unsightly, but it may also point to an underlying problem with drainage – this could be a leaking gutter, or the accumulation of surface water due to a blocked or collapsed drain.

1 A patchy wall with peeling and blistering paint will be a constant distraction, so it is worth taking the time to prepare the wall properly to lessen the risk of the problem recurring.

2 First, untie any climbers or lax shrubs from their support wires or trellis and carefully lay them down on the ground, or draw them to one side. Most will have sufficient flexibility.

3 Using a soft nylon hand brush and a bucket of water containing detergent, scrub off dirt and algae to leave a clean surface. Excessive algal growth may indicate drainage problems.

4 With firm strokes and a circling movement, remove any flakes of loose paint and surface salts with a wire brush. If left behind, these will bubble up and cause the fresh paint to lift and drop off.

5 For more stubborn areas of flaking paint, use a paint scraper to lift away the loose layers. Afterwards, go over the surface with a soft, dry brush to remove dust and any remaining small particles.

6 Seal the wall with a diluted coat of PVA. Apply it liberally. This will help to prevent moisture and salts in the brickwork from lifting the new paint and also acts as an undercoat.

7 Cover the ground with protective sheeting. Then, using a wide brush, paint the wall margins on the top, bottom and sides. This leaves the middle, which you can fill in easily with a roller.

8 A roller and tray designed for applying thick or textured masonry paint will speed up the job. Use a roller with an extension handle, like the one shown here, to avoid using a ladder.

9 You may need to apply a second coat or to touch up the paintwork once the first coat has dried. When dry, reattach the climbers and wall shrubs and review any pruning needs.

Disguising Unattractive Walls

As the most visible surfaces, it is vital to make walls and boundaries as attractive as possible. Having ensured your walls are smart and cared for (see page 17) think about using climbers and wall shrubs to green up and camouflage stark expanses of wall. Learn the requirements of each wall plant so that you can keep them in good condition. Be wary of vigorous climbers such as wisteria, *Clematis montana* and Virginia creeper as these quickly get out of hand.

When planting in front of walls and windows, allow access for window cleaning, painting and pruning. You can use hinged decorative treillage panels to allow access for painting the wall behind. Trellis and bamboo or brushwood screens and panels transform the look of a lacklustre wall or fence. Take care when applying paints, trellis and other decorative façades, as poorly applied elements quickly become eyesores.

Above: *The decorative tile border, tile wall panels and frame of clipped wall shrubs create a dramatic area where otherwise there would have been white walls.*

TRAINING PLANTS AGAINST WALLS

Where space is limited, training plants upwards is an obvious way of maximizing what space is available. It is also a classic way to camouflage less than attractive existing walls and boundaries. Climbers and wall shrubs will usually need some form of strong support, such as trellis panels. These, however, may not always be suitable for certain styles of garden, as they can sometimes look too heavy in a small or confined area. A more discreet option is to use galvanized training wire. A large 'mesh' of horizontal and vertical wires is ideal for climbers with tendrils or twining leaf stems such as passion flower and clematis.

1 Hammer a horizontal line of wedge-shaped vine eyes into the mortar joints (as long as the mortar is sound enough to offer support). Alternatively, for screw-fixings that can be used on walls, fences or posts, first drill the wall with a masonry bit and then plug the holes.

2 Thread the galvanized wire through the hole in the vine eye and wrap it around itself to tie it off. Then thread the wire through the intermediate eyes – set at no more than 1.8m (6ft) intervals. Fasten the wire off firmly after taking up the slack.

3 Set lines of wires around 45cm (18in) apart and attach vertical wires to form a grid-like mesh for climbers to use. Curve long stems along the wires, securing them with soft twine at several points. The closer to the horizontal, the more you encourage flower buds to develop.

ERECTING TRELLIS PANELS

Consider creating a rhythm around your garden room by fixing a repeating pattern of trellis panels. This can have both a decorative and practical purpose. For a secure finish, it is important to fix trellis panels or any climbing mesh on to battens. This also creates a space behind the support, allowing plants to climb more easily. The weight of a mature climbing plant can be substantial, so don't skimp on materials.

1 Mark the position of the spacer battens or lathes. Drill holes in the brickwork (not the mortar joints) using a masonry drill bit. Use wall plugs and galvanized screws.

2 Mark and predrill the battens to fit the holes. Tap in wall plugs until they are flush and screw the battens in. They must hold the trellis at least 2.5cm (1in) away from the wall.

3 Mark and predrill the trellis panel, selecting a cross piece to correspond with the battens. Use galvanized wood screws long enough to fix the panel to the batten.

4 Repeat the previous steps to fix further trellis panels around your garden room. Ensure that they are all at an equal distance from each other and at the same level.

Using Decorative Trellis

Plain and decorative trellis panels make an ornamental addition to the courtyard garden, helping to create depth, texture and colour, and distracting from any less attractive features. Trellis has potential in many styles of garden, and is a classic feature to give a new dimension to a neglected space. The quality of trellis varies. If you can, choose wood that is attached to battens and raised off the ground, which is less likely to rot.

Use a colourful outdoor wood paint or stain to add vibrancy to brick or painted walls, both low-maintenance solutions for colouring wood. It is easier to do this before fixing them, leaning panels against a wall with a protective plastic sheet underneath.

Leave a gap between a planting hole and trellis attached to a wall, to avoid the rain shadow. Use stakes to train your climber up to the base of the panel and then attach the plant stems to it with soft garden twine. Don't use coated wire or rigid plastic ties as these can cut into the plant stems, restricting the flow of sap and causing dieback.

Weaving plant stems in front of and behind the trellis makes pruning more difficult. So, it is better to tie the plant stems only to the panel front.

Above: *Diamond trellis panels have an old-fashioned charm, especially when coupled with posts topped with decorative finials. This trellis panel gives depth and structure to the perimeter of the courtyard.*

PLANTING BASICS

Using plants imaginatively is key to transforming a courtyard. They can disguise or distract from less appealing features, such as lacklustre walls or areas of paving, or just add creative focus. You'll need to identify the plants that thrive in your locality, which soil different plants prefer, how to plant them to maximum effect and overcome problems such as shallow soil.

Above: *Clipped shapes and topiary features add style and a touch of theatre.*

Above: *Tender plants and bedding are high-maintenance options but displays are often the most colourful and eye-catching.*

Plant Preferences

Having identified your soil type and pH range (see page 11), as well as the sunniest and shadiest parts of the plot, you can begin to select which plants to use. So-called *ericaceous* plants require acidic soil in order to thrive. Examples include many woodland shrubs, such as rhododendron and azalea, pieris, camellia and gaultheria, all of which are also useful in shady sites. Some plants enjoy neutral-to-acid soil with a high humus content, but won't die if they don't have acid conditions. These include skimmia, hydrangea (acid soils needed to maintain the blue colouring of some cultivars) and Japanese maple (*Acer palmatum*). Many Mediterranean-type shrubs and herbs, including lavender, prefer alkaline or limy soils, usually coupled with sharp drainage and full sun. Certain vegetables, such as brassicas, also prefer an alkaline soil. In the productive garden you can add lime to raise the pH of the soil.

Above: *Climbers and wall shrubs make the most of available border space.*

PLANTING THROUGH LANDSCAPE FABRIC

For gravel gardens, which are traditionally only sparsely planted, you could consider covering the soil with porous, heavy-duty black landscape fabric topped with a coating of decorative gravel. This has the advantage of suppressing weeds already in the soil, while weed seeds blowing in fail to get their roots down into the ground.

1 Lay the landscape fabric over the prepared soil and peg down all around the edge. Make cross-shaped cuts at each point where you want to locate a plant, shrub or tree.

2 Fold back the four points of the fabric to give you a square large enough to plant in. Dig out the soil until the planting hole is deep enough for the plant's rootball.

3 Set the watered plant in the hole and backfill with soil. Water the plant in well. Ease the black liner back a little, leaving enough space for plant growth.

4 When the planting is complete, clean off the fabric surface and then cover the whole area with gravel to a depth of about 5cm (2in). It is easy to add more plants later.

Pots and Raised Beds

If you don't have borders or exposed soil, you will need to make raised beds or plant in pots, troughs and wall containers. For economy and to ensure long-term success, fill raised beds with good-quality topsoil rather than bags of potting mix, and make sure that any perennial weed roots and seeds have been removed.

Planting up a few pots instantly transforms a dull space. Choose large containers, where possible, as these allow greater planting scope. In addition, use soil-based potting mixes for hardy perennials, shrubs and trees as these will be in their pots for several years.

Busy homeowners with little time to look after a garden planted in containers or with free-draining raised beds should consider installing an automatic irrigation and feeding system to keep their plants in tip-top condition.

Below: *Large planters, the one below made from an old barrel, require less maintenance and offer more scope for imaginative planting than small pots.*

Below: *Even vegetable and herb gardens can be given a contemporary feel, this example showing crisp, timber-walled beds and modern planters.*

PLANTING INTO PAVING

Optimize space by adding plants among paving stones. Low-growing and creeping aromatic herbs and alpines are suitable as they can colonize narrow cracks and crevices. Treading on, or brushing against, the foliage of plants such as thyme and chamomile releases a wonderful fragrance. When laying new areas of paving, set some of the stones at a greater distance apart to create planting areas and fill the gaps with soil rather than mortar.

1 Lift a paving stone in an area where you want to introduce a plant. Against a wall, you have the option to plant climbers and wall shrubs. Avoid planting close to thoroughfares, as plants may grow too large and cause an obstruction.

2 Dig out any cement and hardcore or sand and gravel and replenish the soil by digging it over with a fork and working in some garden compost (soil mix) or an organic soil improver together with some slow-release fertilizer granules.

3 After soaking the plant, excavate a hole large enough to accommodate the rootball and plant, backfilling with soil. Mulch with decorative gravel or grit as a foil for the plants and to keep the foliage dry, or use small cobbles.

CHOOSING A DESIGN

Because of the small scale, and the link to an interior space, a courtyard or terrace can be styled in a similar way to a room. Finding a style or theme is a good starting point and then you need to put together a colour and materials palette. Your reference can include paving catalogues, magazine images, sketches, written notes, as well as a wish list of desired plants and features.

Above: *The neo-classical plinth and treillage are perfect 'period' props.*

QUESTIONS TO ASK YOURSELF

• *Do you want to grow fruits and vegetables, or just ornamentals?*
• *Will you garden in borders or in containers? If you choose the latter, how will you water them?*
• *Would you like a pool or fountain, an outdoor lighting feature or a sculptural focal point?*
• *How about a summerhouse or overhead pergola for privacy?*
• *Might you want to include a barbecue, fire pit or informal seating with tiered decking or terracing?*
• *How will you create access around the garden?*
• *Will you need to camouflage utility areas or section off parts to create secluded corners for entertaining and outdoor dining?*

Above: *The whitewashed wall and potted herbs combined with vibrant purples and pinks create a Mediterranean flavour.*

Above: *A crisp, rectilinear layout perfectly reflects the surrounding architecture.*

Architectural Influences

Aspects of a home's design may form the perfect backdrop for a specific style of garden, but the design of the building and its garden don't have to match slavishly. If, for example, you prefer contemporary looks over Victorian charm or you want your courtyard or terrace to be more country cottage than city chic, try some theatrical stage setting. Cover or camouflage the walls, introduce furniture items, pots and plants, and pick an appropriate colour scheme.

To follow an architectural theme, research the art, architecture and garden styles of the period. You could then select from a number of key features. Don't try to cram in too many visual references, and don't be afraid to mix contrasting styles, for example, combining traditional architectural details and decorative touches with ultra-modern elements.

Evoking a Style

Painting walls and timbers in a co-ordinated colour scheme is an inexpensive way of creating a specific mood or character. Areas used for entertaining and outdoor dining benefit from warm, energizing shades, such as oranges, reds, and vibrant pinks. Use these colours

Above: *If you require a low-maintenance solution, focus on decorative flooring and wall features or other plant-free elements such as sculpture or pebble fountains.*

Right: *Design raised beds and steps to double as impromptu seating or commission bespoke, all-weather furniture.*

sparingly, however, as they will make the garden room feel smaller. Gardens for quiet contemplation should be painted in more muted tones, such as soft blues, greens or pale amethyst, to create a sense of space.

Colour is an essential element of any design theme. When using, perhaps, an Italian Renaissance motif, you might choose tints found in faded frescos – verdigris, dusky rose and aquamarine. In a minimalist setting, consider dove grey, willow green or aubergine. For a Mediterranean feel, try teaming Moroccan blue, ochre or dusty terracotta with limestone or sandstone paving. To create a contemporary spa-style backdrop for a Scandinavian hot tub, you might use eau-de-Nil walls alongside bleached wooden decking, a cream canvas sail awning, pale cobbles and zinc planters filled with grasses.

Right: *The painted decking and wall plaque of the raised seating area give this courtyard the distinct flavour of an interior.*

DRAWING UP A DESIGN

Making a scale plan of the garden will allow you to superimpose any changes to the existing design as well as giving you the ability to try out new features. This is easier than you might think, especially if the courtyard, terrace or patio is composed of rectangular shapes. If you are bringing in contractors, give them a copy of the plan to help with calculating amounts of materials.

Above: *Your design should dovetail with existing features and architectural elements.*

Stage 1: Gather the Data

1 Draw a rough, bird's-eye view sketch of the garden to write measurements on and to help you keep track of progress.
2 Buy a long, flexible measuring tape. Work in metric or imperial, not a mixture of the two. Keep the tape taut by ensuring that one end is firmly fixed. This process is quicker and easier if you have a helper.
3 Record all measurements of the ground area/boundary, including the shape of any wall recesses, bay windows and so on. In addition, mark on the position of drainpipes and drain and manhole covers.
4 Mark the position and dimensions of windows, doors and access points. This will help decide the best place to position features and pathways.

5 Work out the location of plants and features that are away from the boundaries.
6 Record diagonal measurements across the site to help correct the orientation of walls and fences that are not fully perpendicular. The site may not be a perfect rectangle.

Stage 2: Draw the Plan

1 Working with a sheet of graph paper, calculate the scale to fit the longest horizontal and vertical dimensions on the sheet. Make the plan as large as possible so that you have room to try out your ideas. A convenient and typical scale might be 2cm to 1m (or 1in to 3ft).
2 Transfer the measurements to the plan, checking the position of the corners and the angle of boundaries with the diagonal measurements.
3 Mark on the compass points or the extent of shade at different times of the day. Also mark the edge of any

Above: *A scale drawing of the site with the new design in colour helps to visualize the garden and calculate materials.*

overhanging tree canopies or how far a hedge juts out from the boundary line. In addition, mark the position of doors and gates and where they open out into the garden.
4 Draw in points where the garden is overlooked by neighbouring windows and sight lines to focal points outside.

Stage 3: Create a Design

1 Ensure that the lines and subdivisions of your design are in scale with the overall size of the plot and that they link to key architectural points. It helps to superimpose a faint grid of squares on to the plan that relates to points on the house or boundary. For example, the width of the grid squares might be taken from the

Planting notes

1. A small, ornamental tree such as *Prunus subhirella* 'Autumalis Rosea'
2. Evergreen underplanting for shady patch here
3. An exotic evergreen climber for a hot wall, such as *Clematis armandii*
4. *Phormium tenax* as a lush backdrop to the water feature
5. A shade climber for the pergola, such as *Humulus lupulus* 'Aureus'
6, 7 and 8 A selection of large pots, including *Buxus* (clipped box ball) and a Japanese maple
9. Wall-mounted pots with bedding will create a pretty view from the kitchen
10. A self-clinging climber over the wall recess, such as *Hedera*
11. Espalier-trained fruit, such as pear or plum
12. Colourful, easy summer herbaceous plants, such as *Agapanthus*

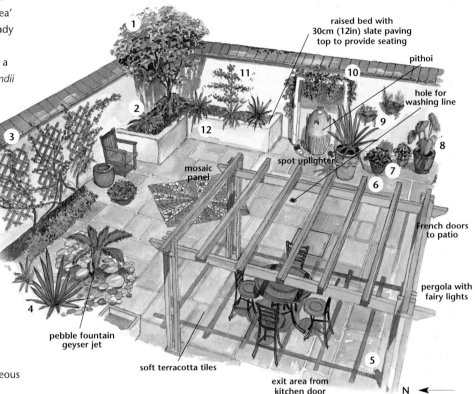

raised bed with 30cm (12in) slate paving top to provide seating

pithoi

hole for washing line

spot uplighter

mosaic panel

French doors to patio

pergola with fairy lights

pebble fountain geyser jet

soft terracotta tiles

exit area from kitchen door

N ←

width of French doors or the distance apart of wall pillars. Rotate this grid on to the diagonal to produce a more dynamic feel.

2 Try out various shapes and patterns within the grid – you can subdivide the squares or superimpose arcs and circles on to it. You need to create a footprint for the garden that relates to the different areas of activity and to the features it will contain, such as an outdoor dining area, a herb garden, an ornamental pool, raised beds or areas of decking.

3 To avoid redrawing as your design changes, cut out the shapes of the key elements in coloured paper and move them around the plan. This will help you find a pattern that both looks in proportion and flows harmoniously.

Right: *Plants, furniture and sculpture are the final touches, added once the hard-landscaping phase has been completed.*

Stage 4: Develop the Plan

1 Once you have the basic shapes, draw on the position of specimen plants as well as the width of retaining walls, the pattern of paving and decking and any changes in level.

2 Use a correspondingly large piece of tracing paper to copy the design from the graph paper, along with any notations. Photocopy it several times. Pick one copy to colour in, or to superimpose a planting plan on. This will be your master copy. Keep the spares for contractors, or to work with out in the garden during the construction and planting phases.

STYLE OPTIONS

How would you like your patio to look?
Here are some ideas about the visual
styles you might want to use when
planning your patio area. Formal Spaces
with clean lines and symmetrical
structures could be filled with fine
specimen plants, elegant ornaments and
decorative features. Mediterranean
Retreats will suit sunshine lovers, spaces
suffused with perfume, and surrounded
by rich colours and collections of potted
plants. Alternatively, inspired by Open-air
Sanctuaries, style your patio space as a
comfortable extension of the interior,
designed for eating, relaxing and
entertaining. Productive Sites, used for
growing your own fruit and vegetables
are always a popular option, so perhaps a
country-style courtyard for cultivating
edible produce is the best answer.
Peaceful Havens are another possibility,
based on relaxation, soothing colours,
gentle planting and informal designs.
Finally, Modern Zones offer clean lines,
structural planting and a delightfully low-
maintenance approach.

Left: *This bright, contemporary patio is simply created with
raised wooden planters painted in vivid colours, a pink
background partition and decking for the walkways.*

FORMAL SPACES

To create a conventional style in your courtyard you can draw on historical architectural influences and simple, reliable materials, such as red brick and natural stone. Classical references play their part in decorative elements made from hand-forged steelwork and cast lead and iron. Planting forms a framework of clipped, dense evergreen, complemented by soft bursts of subtle colour.

Above: *Boxwood (Buxus sempervirens) perfectly sets off the pure white roses.*

Styles and Approaches

A traditional courtyard style can be inspired by different historical periods. A medieval-inspired space, for example, could include a stone folly, masonry with a gothic arch, a simple stone fountain, herbs, and old-fashioned blooms such as musk roses, violets, hollyhocks, larkspur, monkshood and foxgloves. An Arts and Crafts garden could be brought to life with a Lutyens-style bench seat, a bronze resin statue, a stone-paving rill, flaky limestone pillars and paving, clipped topiary and a white and pastel cottage-flower scheme.

To create a Regency style, think of an elegant wirework gazebo with a rambler rose, curving treillage and an antique portico. To conjure up the feel of the Italian Renaissance, choose large, ornate terracotta lemon pots with bay trees, low-clipped box hedging, mellow-coloured gravel and

Above: *The circle of lawn and its curved retaining wall create an intimate seating spot.*

stonework. A loggia and formal rectangular pool, classical statuary, wall masks and architectural plants such as cordyline are more ideas to complete the look.

The visual intention may be a formal, even classical, tableau, but its function should still be considered in terms of contemporary living. Relaxation and entertaining space are all-important features of our lives, and the courtyard garden needs to fulfil differing roles. The inclusion of a dining terrace and a secluded corner dedicated to quiet contemplation will extend the use of the garden and help it to enhance the enjoyment of every day. A classical gazebo or garden folly would create an important architectural element, while also providing cover and privacy for entertaining. A fountain or formal pool can help to cement the design, whilst providing a lively focal point.

Combining Elements

A well-established approach offers reassurance to the novice gardener by setting out a formal layout within which to operate. The manageable scale of the courtyard makes it quite easy to plan, maintain and budget, and it can be created in stages. Hard landscaping is the structural mainstay and its success will depend on the quality of the design detailing and workmanship. Without a strong, basic framework to anchor the design, any subsequent planting will not be completely successful. Clipped evergreen topiary plays a vital part in holding the green structure in place,

while mature trees and shrubs can be included to convey an immediate sense of substance. Incorporating carefully selected planting containers and imposing architectural elements will supply the finishing touches.

A traditional approach does not mean that the garden has to use authentic materials. Newly made and reconstituted pieces that impressively represent the originals can be practical and lightweight, and they are easier on the budget than the real thing. Faux-lead planters made from resin are easy to handle and a blessing for the roof terrace; cast aluminium furniture is a fraction of the weight of cast iron; and tinted cement paving blocks cast in moulds made from old pavements are much less expensive than York stone slabs. The trick in using these products is to retain the integrity of the traditional design thesis and to select the materials with a view to their appearance, quality of manufacture and long-term endurance.

The courtyard can equally support the demands of discerning gardeners who are looking to create a significantly impressive, classical garden. The traditional theme provides the formalized framework in which to indulge a particular interest, whether this is placing rare specimen topiaries, setting out a collection of elegant planting containers or indulging a passion for water.

Right: *Oversized corkscrew stemmed bays (Laurus nobilis) complement this gracious, walled courtyard parterre, both in their scale and ordered alignment.*

MEDITERRANEAN RETREATS

This style of gardening appeals especially to gardeners who enjoy travelling to the sun. Bringing a flavour of the Mediterranean region back to our own gardens prolongs that pleasurable sense of carefree living. As well as including signature plants or hardier look-alikes that are readily available in the summer, you can also find an array of imported pots and planters and garden furniture.

Above: A Marrakesh blue wall highlights the potted citrus and bougainvillea.

Images from Abroad

Although there are similarities between the formal Italian Renaissance-style gardens with their geometric layout, clipped topiaries, aromatic herbs and ornate terracotta pots, the Mediterranean courtyard garden is much more relaxed. The lack of space and simple features results in a more homespun feel, with a jumble of pots and planters – some made from recycled containers – flowers and vegetables, herbs and fruits all vying for growing room. Practicality and productivity can be almost as important as aesthetics, and edible plants that are also attractive frequently substitute for ornamentals. As well as the family courtyard or outdoor room, alive with colourful and fragrant specimens, if space is available small vegetable plots are also lovingly tended. These provide everything from cucumbers, tomatoes, courgettes (zucchini), aubergines (eggplants), beans, potatoes and salads to apricots, peaches, pomegranates and citrus fruits. In a small courtyard you could still attractively incorporate these productive spaces by confining them in rendered raised beds and terracotta pots lined with plastic to conserve moisture.

Planting Choices

With relatively mild winters becoming more common, many gardeners in temperate northern regions can now grow borderline hardy plants outdoors year round without having to bring them under cover at any stage. And, particularly with the shelter that is afforded by courtyard walls and screens, you can try a very wide range of exotics. Heat that is absorbed by paving and brickwork during the day is steadily released into the surrounding air through the night, successfully keeping temperatures a degree or two higher and hopefully above freezing. If you have a frost-free greenhouse or conservatory you can overwinter many more tender plants and start seedlings, bulbs and tubers off earlier in the season to allow them time to mature, flower and fruit in the shorter growing season.

Expanding your planting repertoire by including plants that are commonly used in Mediterranean gardens creates a powerful visual trigger. Large-leaved specimens, such as cannas and hardy bananas, can be combined with succulents and cacti and vibrantly coloured annuals and perennials to great effect, especially when used with terracotta pots, cane furniture and rendered walls. Even dropping in one or two quintessentially Mediterranean plants, such as a potted olive, lemon or bay tree, or planting a grape vine over a pergola suggests a sunnier location. Any of the more tender plants you use may then require some winter protection.

Preparing the Space

Throughout this chapter you will find inspiration for decorating and enlivening your Mediterranean courtyard. Before beginning, it is important to camouflage any parts of the existing surroundings that don't fit in. You could achieve this with paint or render, trellis panels, screens and climbers, pergolas and garden buildings.

Ornamental Detail

The typical rustic Mediterranean courtyard is furnished quite differently to the more opulent Riviera or Moorish style in terms of lamps, tables and chairs, pots and planters, water features, paving, walls and screens.

The following sections examine the different products and materials that you might use and how you can combine them to good effect.

Above: A Greek-island style featuring a compacted clay floor and dusty terracotta.

Right: Whitewashed walls studded with pots and planters, together with an array of houseplants clustered on the terrace, create an oasis effect.

OPEN-AIR SANCTUARIES

A successfully converted outdoor room will give you extra living space and a new extension to your home. This style of courtyard is not so much a visual statement as a way of maximizing living space. Furniture, cooking areas, beds and spas can all have their place, with the planting providing green furnishings and decoration and the hard landscaping new walls and floors.

Above: *Cushioned faux-cane armchairs entice the visitor to an intimate corner.*

Creating a Refuge

On the one hand, in a densely built urban environment, your space may well be defined by boundary walls, which provide a special sense of intimacy and refuge. On the other, an upper level terrace or balcony can give an exciting opportunity to extend your home, perhaps with an open vista of river or landscape. Without the benefit of either – a built enclosure or marvellous views – a simple screen of luxuriant foliage, perhaps in the form of a bamboo hedge or climber-covered screen, can create a personal corner in which to escape with a book.

Surrounding walls provide an excellent opportunity to set a special background theme. The restricted nature of the area allows you to indulge in bold colour statements that would otherwise be overwhelming in a larger garden

Above: *This lightweight aluminium and cane chair provides a shady spot for snoozing.*

space. Walls provide an excellent background from which to display a collection of sculpture or other artefacts. The exotic foliage forms of palm trees and ferns are strikingly thrown into relief against a colour-tinted wall, with lighting available to develop the effect at night.

The garden room becomes a real-life stage set that you can dress in the evening with candles and electric luminaires. Trees become shadowy forms and white flowers gleam eerily, while under-lit water develops a magnified depth and the noise of a fountain takes on a new vibrancy.

Function and Style

The theatrical possibilities provided by an outdoor room give you ample scope to create a special theme for a party or event. Formal, or romantic, let your guests explore the moonlit terrace studded with tiny uplighters set among tall vases of perfumed lilies and play soft music through a sound system of speakers set into the ground. A tented canopy furnished with huge cushions makes an exotic place to relax, especially when it is filled with pots of heavily scented flowers, such as jasmine and gardenia.

If by night the courtyard is all soft lighting and shadows, by day it is brought into focus by clear light and solid form. Colour and texture are now the key, with bright climbers adorning the walls and flowers spilling from containers. Early breakfast takes on a new dimension

when accompanied by birdsong, while later on a vine-covered pergola can shade a simple lunch.

Furniture plays an important role in the outdoor room, both in function and style, and it should reinforce your overall decorating theme. If your taste is for the contemporary, with sleek Italian seating and similarly gleaming kitchen, then your courtyard garden should reflect this. Clean-lined furniture will suitably echo your high-tech interior. Dining outside is a prime function, so lightweight aluminium dining chairs are practical – especially when upholstered in attractively understated nylon mesh fabric, making a perfect modern combination with a slate-topped table. Alternatively, generous cane armchairs and loungers are ideal for relaxing.

Hard-landscaping materials play an important role in creating the structure and should also reinforce the design style. Pale, smooth, sawn limestone combines with deep-toned slate for paving and steps, or fountains and pools. An understated planting scheme, based on foliage form, would complement this well. Slender, swaying grasses, New Zealand flax with its narrow blade-like foliage, interspersed with mauve clusters of *Verbena bonariensis* all contribute to a sense of light airiness.

Right: *Narrow timber slats create side screens and a canopy as an enclosure for this elegantly coordinated, modern roof terrace.*

PRODUCTIVE SITES

A country-style courtyard is the perfect setting for combining edible produce with colourful cut flowers for the house. What could be more satisfying than preparing a meal from home-grown vegetables and fruit, with freshly cut herbs to add zest and colour to both hot dishes and salads, with the added pleasure of arranging your own garden flowers for the table?

Above: *Aubergines, squashes and beetroot vie for space with nasturtiums.*

Design and Selection

Creating a flower-filled, countrified garden space calls for a natural approach to the design of the courtyard as well as to the selection of appropriate plants and materials. Aim for a relaxed, informal approach to its planting, with just enough 'edge' to lift the design into the realms of something special.

Divide the space up with paths surfaced in crunchy gravel and edge them with tumbling herbs. Extend the scope and dimensions of the available space by introducing vertical elements using vine-clad structures, such as arbours, screens and arches.

There is an opportunity to grow a wealth of traditional cottage garden plants, including hollyhocks and lupins, delphiniums and columbines, with roses underplanted with catmint for a soft, final touch. The planting can appear random

and unplanned, mixing a riot of colours, textures and scents, or it can be organized into groups of toning colours and harmonizing shades.

To make the most of a restricted space, set vegetable plots within a framework of decorative planting. This not only maintains interest for the greater part of the year but also protects produce from pest damage by drawing in natural predators such as hoverflies and lacewings.

Climbing roses, honeysuckle and golden hop can all be trained on walls and fences or over arbours and screens. Colourful climbing squashes look impressive, too. Introduce a Mediterranean flavour to a sunny spot by combining tall-growing globe artichokes with underplantings of scented lavender, thyme and sage.

Apples can be trained along stakes and wires to make low screens and divisions. Dwarf plums and cherry trees will deliver fruit to make jams and pies, while in warmer areas you can train peaches and apricots against a south-facing wall.

Where space is at a premium, you will be amazed at just how much edible produce you can grow in pots and containers. Select the largest pot or container you can find to give enough space for good root growth and plenty of water and nutrients. Discarded industrial containers, such as oil drums, make excellent planters, but ensure that they are thoroughly cleaned before use.

Generously proportioned, purpose-built wooden planters and

Above: *Tomatoes grow well in pots against a sunny wall, but need regular attention.*

troughs can be placed along walls where they will benefit from the warmth and shelter. Alternatively, use them to create divisions in the garden. Raised beds make excellent planting areas where there is inadequate depth or quality of natural soil. Form the side walls from heavy timber planks or railway sleepers and fill with a mixture of existing soil and new compost (soil mix), incorporating lots of well-rotted farmyard or horse manure to make instant and easy-to-work beds.

Seed Varieties

The choice of flower and vegetable seeds to grow has never been wider, with many new and improved choices to make trial and selection a real seasonal treat. Old-fashioned vegetable varieties make it possible to grow food that you could never find in the shops. Striped tomatoes, pink carrots and black beans are among the tempting and colourful choices to include in your home-grown vegetable dishes. To make the most of a small space, use vegetables that are best picked fresh, such as runner (green) beans, salads, baby carrots or cherry tomatoes.

When it comes to fruit, there are many new, so-called 'patio' varieties, dwarf trees such as apples, apricots, peaches, pears and cherries that quickly become the real jewels of any small or container garden.

Right: *This courtyard combines vegetables, fruit and flowers for decoration. Cane wigwams, which will be clothed in colourful climbing beans, add vertical interest.*

PEACEFUL HAVENS

A contemplative courtyard should feel natural and understated, ordered but free-flowing. It should stimulate your senses, drawing you in mentally and physically, inviting the discovery of lush greenery with the life-giving moisture and oxygen it brings. It will provide a place to lose yourself among the sounds of breeze-rustled foliage, trickling water and birdsong.

Above: *Swathes of grasses and soft-flowering perennials create a soothing mood.*

Lush Greenery

A dense covering of plants will help to create a sense of privacy in the contemplative courtyard – and that sense of being away from other people's notice can be a rare and precious asset in a busy urban setting.

The appropriate choice of plants can create a living screen to enclose your space, principally achieved by building up layers of sculptural greenery. For example, try placing tall bamboos at the rear of your space to create an impenetrable barrier and then gradually reduce the height and bulk of the planting in front. In this way, you introduce a new dimension – the usual height and spread, but also the third dimension of depth.

Impressively architectural, tree ferns provide a dappled canopy of long, arching fronds, while clipped

Above: *A symbolic Zen garden suggesting mountains, forests, fields and seascape.*

evergreen shrubs, such as *Ligustrum* sp. and tailored pines, will introduce bold outline and form.

To soften the near distance, plant swathes of delicate grasses to sway and rustle in the breeze, with a low underplanting of perennials, ferns and mosses at their base. By mixing sculptural evergreens with deciduous shrubs and perennials, you can form a miniature landscape that will reflect the changing seasons, from delicate spring bulbs and blossoms to fiery autumn tints and with the skeletal outline of bare branches in the winter.

Hard Landscaping and Structures

Provide your contemplative courtyard garden with layers of structure and textural interest through the elements of hard landscaping you introduce. A small space will be enlarged by even small changes of level. Ensure, however, that any such changes in level are not so subtle that they become trip hazards.

Link different levels with steps that are slow and shallow, meandering into sinuous paths to lead you gradually through the garden, allowing plenty of time for you to appreciate your surroundings. Crunchy gravel or layers of slate chippings look informal and introduce an interesting texture to contrast with the softer forms of the surrounding foliage.

Structures should blend sympathetically with the natural design approach. Create them from textural and sensuous raw materials, using natural wood and stone in a

form that is close to its raw, natural state. Timber sleepers (ties) and reclaimed driftwood combine well for steps and retaining walls, while blocks of natural stone, as well as being practical elements, can be introduced as sculptural forms in their own right.

Observation Points

So that you can appreciate your surroundings, provide comfortable seating at various points, especially to enjoy a special aspect of the outside space. A Zen-style viewing garden could make an interesting central feature. This could be designed in the classically cool style, with an area of raked gravel to be punctuated by a group of specially selected rocks and minimal, evergreen planting. A solid bamboo fence would provide a suitable, though austere, backdrop. Alternatively, a screen of living bamboo would offer a valuable green relief, without distracting from the main feature.

The Power of Water

Water in the garden will never fail to relax and invigorate both mind and body. A still, quiet pool provides a cool, clear space that will capture shadows, reflections and glints of sunlight. If you border it with willowy water plants, then birds and other wildlife will be attracted to drink and bathe.

Right: *Some uprights in this timber post screen are painted an ox-blood colour, complemented by the planting of silver-leafed helichrysum and bronze dracaena palms.*

MODERN ZONES

A contemporary courtyard demands bold geometry of form, clean textures and crisp planting to create a garden with dynamic character and structure. A sensible approach is to use a formal design that echoes the appearance of the surrounding architecture, creating visual and physical links between the house and the hard landscaping outside.

Above: *Brilliant red and white Perspex is softened with the leaves of a giant gunnera.*

Reinterpreting the Classic

A contemporary garden will often be based on a classic formal design, using orthodox principles of order and arrangement, but reinterpreted in a fresh and original way. New types of construction materials make complex structures possible, and together with the use of bold, brilliant colours and unexpected textures, have turned many established gardening ideas on their head.

Traditional garden design principles can be used to formulate the basic structure, for example sculpting a hedge or designing a partition to mirror the form of a window, echo the scale of a door or follow the line of a roof. This approach helps to create a complementary external reflection of the building's proportion and style.

Above: *Weatherproofed screen prints introduce an unusual sculptural dimension.*

Modern Materials

The use of non-traditional and experimental materials will be a key feature of a contemporary space. Concrete is used to make polished, free-standing walls and sweeping steps, while stainless steel leaves behind its industrial roots and is translated into canopies, screens and sculpture; crushed, coloured glass or even crumbled, recycled rubber may take the place of traditional ornamental mulch. Coloured Perspex (Plexiglass) screens divert the eye and paving is employed to play visual tricks with perspective. A water sculpture created from fragments of glass can sparkle and glint in sunlight, while at night it can appear to glow with the help of carefully planned lighting.

The modern courtyard allows the urban dweller to have fun with a quirky selection of containers and associated planting, as well as in the choice of cutting-edge sculpture. Choosing intriguing, abstract pieces of art brings a whole new emotional dimension to the design, allowing for the expression of personal tastes and preferences.

Planting Choices

Since modern gardens rely heavily on architectural structure, when creating a smaller-scale courtyard scheme you need to retain the overall balance of the space. Too often, designers concentrate so much on the hard landscaping elements that the overall philosophy of the garden is lost. Crisp, minimal designs can be delightfully cool, while some modern materials are quirkily amusing, but also remember the value of planting to create ambiance, energy and character.

A clean-lined space provides a neutral vehicle to show off the wow factor of contemporary planting. The form, texture, colour and movement of trees, shrubs and perennials offers a huge palette of possibilities.

Low maintenance might be a requirement, but a balance can be struck. Tailored evergreens will normally be used to hold together the framework of the planting design; evergreens keep their leaves throughout the year and usually require a twice-annual trim. However, seasonal change is a valuable factor in planting design, so easy-care deciduous species should be considered, too.

A strong visual statement can be achieved using lines of identical trees, trained as standards with a clear trunk. Underplant them with clipped blocks of single-species low evergreens to create a living architectural statement of huge character. Formal cubist-style arrangements of this sort can be chosen from a huge diversity of planting, including grasses and bamboo, or seasonal flowers and bulbs, to change the look of the design throughout the year.

Right: *This sophisticated urban courtyard has permeable paving and is designed to divert water from the porch to irrigate a raised bed and eliminate water run off.*

CASE STUDIES

Here you will find six fascinating case studies of patio gardens, each example bringing individual features to life in a three-dimensional context. The components within each case study include an illustrated garden plan, practical information on hard landscaping, garden features and plants, and two step-by-step sequences explaining how to create elements shown in the location. Planting approaches include the use of clipped evergreens, architectural plants, draught-tolerant succulents, foliage effects, and co-ordinated containers. Among the illustrated hard-landscaping options are gravel pathways, tiled steps, quarry tiles and slate paths. Practical instructions about other garden features explain how to create a hot-pile compost bin, install a wall fountain or build a raised pool. All this means you can use this section as a source of ideas for your own patio.

Left, clockwise from top left: *This enclosed city courtyard is divided into self-contained areas; A gravel base and stone paving is a good solution for a productive patio; A rustic, Tuscan style with architectural planting defines this space; Comfortable seating will increase the pleasure of the outdoors; Box balls create tailored forms that are ideal for symmetrical arrangements; Blue-grey* Festuca glauca *is planted in a mass in these raised beds.*

FORMAL TERRACE

This tiny courtyard forms the entrance to a private house. It is enclosed by high screen walls and dense, evergreen foliage, with a solid door with an impressive classical portico to the neighbouring street adding a theatrical touch of grandeur. Familiar themes hold the look together, with repeating spheres of clipped topiary in different sizes.

Above: *Perfectly clipped balls of box (Buxus sempervirens) give continuity of form.*

The overwhelmingly striking feature of this terrace is the mass of oversized planting that makes a bold, sculptural statement in its own right. The planting is composed entirely of evergreen subjects, which provide structure and interest throughout the year. Tall screens of mature, dark-green ivy surmount the walls, increasing the sense of privacy. A bare splash of a red rambling rose flashes through from the sunny side facing the street.

The garden otherwise tells a very clear colour story that helps to maximize the impression of space. It is comprised of painted white walls and fences, the painted gate and matching trellis panels piercing the ivy screens. A pale stone table with an amusing pair of rusty chairs with a cat motif form the centrepiece. A terracotta wall fountain (see installation method described on page 55) and small pots echo the material of the paving slabs, which are laid in a diagonal grid pattern to extend the sense of perspective with darker, contrasting edging that gives the paving a 'woven-carpet' feel.

The evergreen plants, including *Buxus, Ligustrum* and *Prunus lusitanica*, are clipped into curving shapes that are repeated throughout the garden. The sculptural hedges have a rounded profile and all the specimen topiaries are clipped into balls. Even though the planting is entirely of evergreen plants, the variety of different species provides contrasting leaf shape, texture and colour tone.

The garden plan for this formal terrace, shown overleaf, demonstrates clearly how the symmetrical layout is emphasized by paired plantings. Shade-tolerant ivy and camellia-clad walls create a leafy backdrop for the tiled central area. The green architecture includes large camellia (see planting method described on page 41), and Portuguese laurel standards and cloud-pruned specimens flanking the doorway.

Above: *This cat-embellished chair adds a sense of fun to the strictly formal setting.*

Right: *The terracotta tiles create an intimate sitting area in the garden, surrounded by a wall of dense, evergreen foliage that protects it from the street.*

CREATING A FORMAL TERRACE

Flooring:
• *Use just one or two hard landscaping materials throughout the scheme.*
• *Research classical patterns and incorporate them into the design.*
• *Contrasting dark and light tones helps to reinforce the layout.*
• *Use layout patterns to emphasize direction and changes of level.*

Plants and Containers:
• *Large clipped topiaries reinforce the classical theme and give a sculptural feel.*

• *Choose a core of evergreen planting to hold the structure and appearance right through the year.*
• *Maintain one shape as a clipping motif – round, square or pyramid – to preserve a consistent appearance.*

Structures and Furniture:
• *Keep to a single theme.*
• *Materials for focal points such as furniture or sculpture should fit within the main palette of colour or texture to maintain a consistent theme.*

• *Use bold statements, which help to give an impression of space.*
• *Disguise any awkward or ill-fitting features by painting them out in a scheme colour.*

Ornament and Water Features:
• *Use a neutral colour palette with a maximum of three co-ordinating elements.*
• *Use classical imagery throughout, from flowers to mythological creatures, to maintain the traditional look.*

FORMAL TERRACE GARDEN PLAN

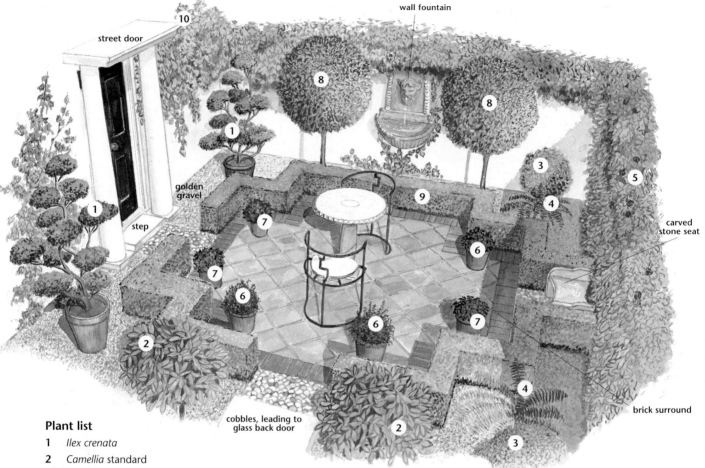

street door

10

wall fountain

golden gravel

step

carved stone seat

cobbles, leading to glass back door

brick surround

Plant list

1 *Ilex crenata*
2 *Camellia* standard
3 *Buxus sempervirens*
4 *Polystichum* fern
5 *Camellia japonica* hedge, with *Hedera helix* and *Rosa* growing over
6 *Lonicera nitida*
7 *Hedera helix* (topiary)
8 *Prunus lusitanica*
9 *Buxus sempervirens* 'Suffruticosa'
10 *Hedera helix*

Above: *Japonica camellias have a glossy green foliage and work well as an informal hedge, with a dramatic flower display in the colder part of the year.*

Left: *The formal, evergreen shapes of the* Buxus *give a clean-edged profile and a monumental presence.*

Below: Prunus lusitanica *is formed into two tall formal standards, and* Buxus sempervirens *is shaped into two low sculptural globes, giving the courtyard an impressive symmetry.*

Above: *Ivy* (Hedera helix) *tumbles over the* Camellia japonica *hedge.*

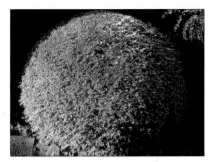

Above: Lonicera nitida *'Baggesen's Gold' is a honeysuckle here used as sphere topiary.*

Above: Polystichum aculeatum, *or hard shield fern, thrives in light shade.*

INSTALLING A WALL FOUNTAIN

Wall fountains make the most of a small volume of water and are ideal for courtyard, basement and roof gardens where there isn't enough room for a stand-alone pool. This design uses a sunken, covered reservoir.

1 Select a traditional wall mask with a tubular metal waterspout already fitted.
2 Dig out the sunken reservoir and insert a rigid liner with a removable metal grill cover. These sets are commonly available from water garden specialists.
3 Thread the delivery pipe from the pump in the reservoir through and then angled up behind a double wall. Drill the holes using a masonry bit, switching to the hammer action on your drill.
4 Connect the pipe from the pump and the copper pipe in the mask to the pipe behind the wall with right-angle bends.

To do this, use a plumber's pipe bender or pipe spring.
5 Secure the mask and spill basin below to the wall with large fixing bolts. Drill the holes, using the appropriate masonry drill bit, and insert wall plugs before screwing in place.
6 Fill the reservoir with water and connect the pump to a waterproof socket approved by an electrician.
7 Test the flow rate, adjusting the tap on the pump until the desired effect is achieved. Replace the reservoir mesh and cover it with cobbles.

WALL FOUNTAIN CROSS-SECTION

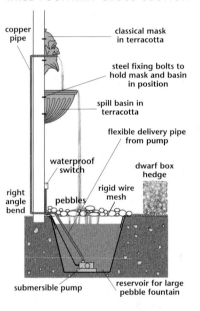

- copper pipe
- classical mask in terracotta
- steel fixing bolts to hold mask and basin in position
- spill basin in terracotta
- flexible delivery pipe from pump
- waterproof switch
- dwarf box hedge
- right angle bend
- pebbles
- rigid wire mesh
- submersible pump
- reservoir for large pebble fountain

PLANTING CAMELLIA

Camellias thrive in containers, particularly smaller, compact cultivars. Restrict growth by pruning after flowering. They are ericaceous, or lime-hating, plants, so use an ericaceous compost (soil mix). Regular watering is essential during the growing season. If you live in a hard-water area use rainwater collected in a water butt.

1 Use terracotta or stone containers for these heavy plants. Place crocks over the holes and begin filling with ericaceous compost (acid soil mix) with added loam. Mix some grit in to very large pots.

2 Soak the plant's root-ball (roots) before planting. Remove from the pot and check that the compost depth is correct. The final level should be about 2.5cm (1in) below the pot rim.

3 If the plant is pot bound, gently tease out some of the thickest roots with your fingers or a hand fork. Fill in around the root-ball, firm with your hands and add a support stake if needed.

4 Use a slow-release fertiliser for ericaceous (acid-loving) plants. Top dress with a layer of grit or gravel. Place the camellia in its final position, such as against a shady north-facing wall.

TUSCAN HIDEAWAY

With a predominance of terracotta and sepia tones and a design of rustic simplicity, this courtyard brings to mind an old country farmhouse surrounded by olive groves, vineyards and fields of lavender. The walls of the house ensure that half the garden is in shade during the hottest part of the day and in summer the tiled pool surrounded by potted ferns becomes a cooling focus.

Above *The bright foliage of* Houttuynia cordata *smells of Seville oranges.*

Above: *The steps into the courtyard are decorated with clay pots and bright blooms.*

The roughly rendered walls and raised beds of this courtyard have been made from inexpensive breeze (cinder) blocks. The boundary walls are topped with reclaimed clay roof tiles, but plain curved pantiles would give a more informal look. The warm apricot colour wash makes an ideal backdrop for the verdigris-effect table and chair and the blue tiled pool. The same tile motif has been stencilled on to the wall and distressed to create the illusion of age.

Another simple technique is the floor treatment. The mellow gravel, laid on top of well-consolidated hardcore, picks up on the wall colours and makes a satisfying crunching sound underfoot. Exterior-quality floor tiles are laid in a simple grid pattern within the gravel to create textural interest.

Other understated decorative elements include the amphora and box and cotton lavender topiaries in weathered terracotta pots. Architectural planting accents add to the Mediterranean atmosphere and include young olive trees (*Olea europaea*), a variegated yucca, Canary Island date palm (*Phoenix canariensis*), New Zealand phoenix palm (*Phoenix sylvestris*), New Zealand flax (*Phormium tenax*) and a hardy fig. Frost is rare in such city courtyards and gaps in the raised beds have been filled with conservatory plants.

The garden plan overleaf portrays an intimate garden room designed as a relaxing space. It can be accessed from the upper floor by an external stairway and on ground level through French doors, behind the pool, which can be left open in warm weather. The tiled pool, with Moorish colours and patterns, provides a tranquil focus for the garden. No serious gardening is required here, but spare plants, watering cans, weatherproof garden equipment and compost (soil mix) can be hidden behind the screening wall.

Right: *Low walls, capped with old terracotta tiles, form a textural screen around this Mediterranean courtyard.*

CREATING A TUSCAN HIDEAWAY

Flooring:
• *Use beach shingle or flint chippings with contrasting areas of quarry tiles or rough stone slabs.*
• *Consider sandstone paving with inserts of terracotta/clay setts or simple pebble mosaics.*

Walls:
• *Render brick or breeze (cinder) block walls and raised beds and apply a dusty terracotta paint effect.*
• *Cap boundary walls with terracotta pantiles or rugged stone slabs.*

Pots and Containers:
• *Choose plain terracotta pots such as traditional Cretan pots and amphora.*
• *Fix pots to the wall using wire.*

Planting:
• *Select evergreen foundation plants such as slender Italian cypress, sweet bay, yucca, phormium, hardy palms, olive trees and simple topiary forms.*
• *Use drought-tolerant succulents and geraniums in pots.*
• *In the shade, use box,* Fatsia japonica *and ferns.*

• *Raised beds around the walls provide warm, well-drained conditions for herbs, salads and Mediterranean climbers.*

Structures and Furniture:
• *Use simple wood and metal folding furniture for a more rustic feel.*
• *Try mosaic table-tops, painted and distressed wooden furniture, old wirework or wicker chairs.*

Water Features
• *A small raised pool or wall fountain provides cooling relief in summer.*

TUSCAN HIDEAWAY GARDEN PLAN

storage space
for pots and
young plants

wall planter

verdigris
wall mask

wall of house

gravel

steps

site of
wall stencil
(see page 83
and opposite)

Greek-style
amphora

Plant list

1   *Rodgersia aesculifolia*
2   *Osmunda regalis*
3   *Houttuynia* 'Chameleon'
4   *Dryopteris cristata*
5   *Phormium tenax*
6   *Osmanthus x burkwoodii*
7   *Buxus sempervirens*
    'Suffruticosa'
8   *Buxus sempervirens*
9   *Leucothoe fontenesiana*
    'Rainbow'
10 *Phoenix canariensis*
11 *Olea europaea*
12 *Yucca gloriosa* 'Variegata'
13 *Ficus* 'Brown Turkey'
14 *Colocasia* 'Black Magic'
15 *Thymus* 'Pink Chintz'
16 *Carissa macrophylla*
17 *Santolina*
    chamaecyparissus
18 *Dryopteris erythrosora*
19 *Pelargonium*

Above: *The soft mellow finish of the low walls provides a subtle background for the planting of smooth, spherical topiary as well as spiky yuccas and phormiums.*

Above *Common box (Buxus sempervirens) is closely clipped into a rounded shape.*

Above: *Wild thyme (Thymus 'Pink Chintz') is situated at the base of the olive tree bed.*

Above: *The Royal Fern (Osmunda regalis) softens the edges of the pool.*

Above: *Cotton lavender works in a pot, or as ground cover.*

CREATING A RAISED POOL

Installing a pool with raised sides gives prominence to the pool, and allows you to perch on the edge. The one shown here is freestanding but you could build it against a wall and combine it with a waterspout.

1 Mark out the pool. Level and compact the area and dig out a square-shaped trench for the wall footings (30cm/12in deep). Add compacted hardcore topped with 20cm (8in) of concrete and level off.
2 Build up the walls of the pool using breeze (cinder) blocks cemented with mortar. Check with a spirit level that the sides are level and perpendicular.
3 Once the walls are done, fill the base with 5cm (2in) of soft sand and tamp down.

4 Use a piece of black butyl rubber pond liner to make a waterproof inner, folding it at the corners and generously overlapping the blocks. Once the water is added the liner will adjust its position.
5 Roughly render the walls of the pool, or apply frostproof tiles using waterproof, exterior-quality tile grout. Keep the flexible liner in place and form a seat by cementing on overlapping coping stones or tiles.

MEDITERRANEAN POOL CROSS-SECTION

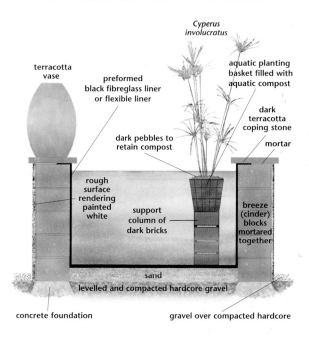

Cyperus involucratus

terracotta vase

preformed black fibreglass liner or flexible liner

aquatic planting basket filled with aquatic compost

dark terracotta coping stone

mortar

dark pebbles to retain compost

rough surface rendering painted white

support column of dark bricks

breeze (cinder) blocks mortared together

sand

levelled and compacted hardcore gravel

concrete foundation

gravel over compacted hardcore

CREATING A WALL STENCIL

Wall tiles were often used to add colour and texture to Moorish courtyard gardens, but it can be difficult to acquire authentic tiles. This technique enables you to recreate the effect purely in paint. A tile design from a magazine was simplified and enlarged and traditional paint colours were softened and distressed to create an aged effect.

1 Transfer a design to oiled manilla stencil card and cut out the sections to be coloured with a craft knife. Include a fine margin to define the tile shape.

2 Fix the stencil to the wall. Use three shades of artist's acrylic paint or stencil paint to stipple the paint on and build up darker shading on the petals.

3 Arrange the tiles to create a random pattern. Line up the stencils so that the same gap is used between each. Remove the stencil.

4 When dry, go over selected tile motifs with fine-grade sandpaper to create an aged effect. Seal using exterior-quality, colourless matt varnish.

MOROCCAN NIGHTS

This colourful, exotic location combines different levels, strong architectural features and separate areas for dining and relaxing. The sumptuous detailing provides not only visual stimulation but also elegant comfort. It is the quintessential outdoor room, with the styling and purpose mirroring the architecture of an interior. But instead of an enclosed ceiling, here the sky takes its place.

Above: *Mounds of ethnic rugs and cushions bring colour to a bench.*

A vibrant Moroccan theme reverberates through this sensual courtyard, lushly planted with climbers, architectural palms and colourful, perfumed flowers. Castellated parapets and Arabian-style keyhole doorways define the high, enclosing walls. Rendered and painted a soft pink to match the pale terracotta paving, both are relieved by the blue and gold mosaic-tiled surface cladding and floor insets.

An intimate, plant-filled alcove enclosed by tall, tile-clad columns provides a private seating area set with a comfortable bench, while in a quiet viewing niche there is a metal table and chairs for relaxed dining and entertaining. The table is set with opulent blue and gold crockery, while the bench, invitingly covered with colourful rugs and velvet cushions, is the perfect place to pass a few idle hours or to relax with friends after an alfresco, candle-lit meal. The alcove also has a marble bowl balanced on a tiled plinth to provide a gentle splash of water. The reservoir holding the bowl is shallow and finished in ceramic glazed tiles.

Vertical interest is further provided by changes of level, with tiled steps leading down to a lower terrace. The main point of interest here is a dramatically long, formal pool. A tall, wrought-iron minaret, based on the minaret at the Hassan II mosque in Casablanca, Morocco, dominates this. Beneath, on a submerged plinth, sits an elegant amphora planted with an exotic *Agave americana* 'Variegata'. The pool's still water is ideal for growing the white water lily *Nymphaea* 'Gladstoniana'. The pool is crossed by two square stepping-stones, bringing the viewer closer to the water.

The garden plan for this Moroccan courtyard is shown overleaf, along with instructions for building a flight of steps and tiling step risers.

Right: *A keyhole opening gives access to the plant-filled inner courtyard, with its tall pillars clad in glazed deep blue and yellow tiles.*

Above: *High walls in soft terracotta provide a serene backdrop to the dining area.*

CREATING A MOROCCAN COURTYARD

Flooring:
• *Pave the floor with terracotta tiles, using decorative tiles as relief insets.*
• *Create changes of level with steps tiled in mosaics.*

Walls and Screens:
• *Render with cement stucco tinted in rich warm colours.*
• *Use tiling to add decorative relief to vertical elements.*
• *Folding perforated screens made from cedar or wrought iron introduce decorative vertical elements.*

Plants and Containers:
• *Use tall palm trees to introduce strong foliage form.*
• *Add architectural interest with curvy Ali Baba pots made from terracotta.*
• *Citrus trees, stephanotis and hibiscus add an exotic touch for summer time.*

Structures and Furniture:
• *Build high architectural blockwork walls for seclusion and intimacy.*
• *Add castellations or crenellations to provide a themed decoration.*
• *Use arched and curved shapes.*

• *Choose wrought-iron chairs and mosaic-topped tables.*

Ornament and Water Features:
• *Create key-hole wall niches for lanterns and other ornaments.*
• *Water features should have a pool with a central fountain.*
• *If you have room, add channels or rills.*

Lighting:
• *Introduce delicate spangles of light with lighting strings.*
• *Use filigree candle lanterns on tables.*

MOROCCAN NIGHTS GARDEN PLAN

wrought-iron minaret

rendered block wall

Moroccan-style pillars

21

24

23

22

21

1

2

20

18

6

19

12

13

Amphora jar

4

15

3

5

14

17

16

10

steps

6

Long pool

9

8

tiled step risers

7

11

Left: *An open niche reduces the impact of the high wall and provides a decorative opportunity with this potted agave.*

Below: *A small space can appear larger when changes in level are incorporated. Wide, gentle steps provide the perfect introduction to the long formal pool below.*

Plant list

1   *Chamaerops humilis*
2   *Phormium tenax* 'Purpureum Group'
3   *Achillea filipendulina* 'Cloth of Gold'
4   *Rosa* 'Irish Eyes'
5   *Griselinia littoralis*
6   *Helenium* 'Wyndley'
7   *Canna* 'Roitelet'
8   *Rosmarinus officinalis*
9   *Convolvulus cneorum*
10 *Phygelius* 'African Queen'
11 *Nymphaea* 'gladstoneana'
12 *Sisyrinchium californicum*
13 *Agave americana*
14 *Heuchera micrantha* var. *diversifolia* 'Palace Purple'

15 *Tagetes* Gem Series
16 *Artemisia* 'Boughton Silver'
17 *Hakonechloa macra* 'Aureola'
18 *Agave americana* 'Variegata'
19 *Fatsia japonica*
20 *Rosa* 'Snowball'
21 *Arundo donax*
22 *Onopordum acanthium*
23 *Cercis canadensis* 'Forest Pansy'
24 *Cytisus battandieri*

Above: *Luxurious cushions help to soften the effect of walls and tiling.*

Above: *Table settings are strongly co-ordinated with the overall theme.*

Above: *Orange and purple planting makes a good foil for the terracotta paintwork.*

BUILDING STEPS

Changes in level add interest to a small garden and a shallow flight of steps can be created fairly easily without the help of a professional builder. Plan the steps carefully and choose materials that will integrate naturally with their surroundings. Draw up a cross-section on squared paper first and then peg out the area for construction.

FLIGHT OF STEPS CROSS-SECTION

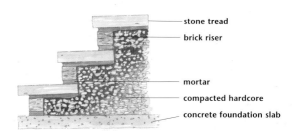

- stone tread
- brick riser
- mortar
- compacted hardcore
- concrete foundation slab

1 Measure the overall height and width of the area where the steps will be located. This should be at least 1.5m (5ft). The height of each riser should be 10–15cm (4–6in) only and the depth of each tread 30–40cm (12–18in).
2 Excavate and lay a concrete foundation under the area of the steps, extending it slightly in front of the first riser. When the concrete is

dry, lay a course of bricks bedded in mortar to form the first riser.
3 Infill behind with hardcore and consolidate firmly by tamping it down with a wooden post.
4 Lay a mortar bed to the depth of the tread over the bricks and hardcore. Set the stone tread so that it projects over the riser by about 2.5cm (1in). Check

the level of the slabs with a spirit (carpenter's) level to ensure that there is a slope to provide a run-off for rainwater.
5 Spread a layer of mortar along the back of the tread and lay a course of bricks over the slab for the second riser.
6 Infill with hardcore, and lay the stone tread as before.

7 Continue building, checking the levels with a spirit level to ensure a slight slope for water run-off. Make sure that the top tread finishes level with the upper ground surface.
8 Glazed ceramic tiles to suit the scheme can be mortared to the riser of each step.

CREATING TILED STEP RISERS

Sophisticated detailing, such as these tiled risers, helps to blur the distinction between indoor and garden rooms, and can link up with other features, colours and design themes – in this example, a Moorish motif of blue and gold.

1 Clean the steps with a brush. Arrange the tiles equidistantly along the step to calculate the spacing and then fix each one with quick-bonding, exterior-quality tile cement.

2 Mix up some mortar, adding sufficient water to create a stiff consistency. Using a small grouting trowel, push the mortar into the gaps between, above and below the tiles.

3 Make the mortar smooth and level with the tiles except along the top; angle the mortar there back under the slab to minimize water retention and staining. Repeat along the bottom.

4 Use a damp cloth wrapped around your forefinger to carefully wipe off excess mortar. Then use a clean, dry cloth to buff the surface of the tiles, removing any smudges.

EDIBLE BOUNTY

This unusual potager is set against a lush background of exotic tree ferns and Australian gum trees, which together provide protection from the wind and shade from the heat of the sun. A setting as dramatic as this demands an equally bold selection of complementary and exuberant vegetables and herbs to create a beautiful yet entirely practical garden space.

Above: *Raised planting beds are made here from sheets of exterior-grade plywood.*

The planting areas of this potager have been devised as a series of raised beds to provide the benefits of deep, good-quality soil. The extra soil depth helps to overcome the problems associated with cultivation in a generally dry environment.

Above: *This decorative chicken will never disturb the crop of alpine strawberries.*

The beds are manageably sized to simplify access and maintenance and their curved, organic shapes integrate well into the wild surroundings. The beds are imaginatively contained by sheets of painted exterior-grade plywood, riveted together and painted earth red. The pathways, generously wide to allow wheelbarrows to navigate easily, are covered with gravel spread over compacted earth and hardcore.

Bold, rustic timbers have been used to construct the sturdy, cabin-style shed. An essential, shady veranda, roofed with traditional corrugated iron and supported on tree-trunks, has been incorporated to one side. Outside, furniture has been fashioned from pieces of reclaimed driftwood. Rambling orange nasturtiums provide ground cover as well as a colourful foil to the bleached timbers, and the whole effect is one of barely tamed domesticity in a savage environment.

The exuberant winter planting introduces bold form as well as vitamins and includes varieties of cabbage, kale and broad (fava) beans. Climbing varieties are supported on suitably curvy, local tree branches.

An abundance of rampant herbs, including parsley, chives and thyme, bursts over the edges of the beds. A curled-up hosepipe hints at water delivered from a sheltered, above-ground tank that captures every drop of precious rainfall.

The garden plan for this potager, shown overleaf, portrays a cultivated space, a productive oasis within a wild landscape. Also included on page 53 are two practical features, one on creating a hot-pile compost bin and the other explaining how to lay tiles on gravel to give a practical floor on which to cultivate your produce.

Right: *Every inch of space is utilized here with the exuberant planting of pungent aromatics and heavily textured kale.*

CREATING A SUCCESSFUL POTAGER

Soil Preparation:
- *The soil must be deep and have good structure and texture.*
- *Incorporate plenty of bulky organic manure to improve light and sandy soils or heavy clay soils.*
- *Remove all perennial weeds before starting soil preparation.*
- *Cultivate the soil with a mechanical device or dig it over thoroughly to improve its structure.*
- *Remove stones and rake the surface to a fine tilth before seed sowing.*

Screens and Divisions:
- *Sunshine should be available for most of the day, but in extreme conditions, shade trees or other types of screening should be in place.*
- *Grow fruit and vegetables on walls and other vertical structures. Attach a trellis or wires for climbers such as runner (green) beans or gourds.*

Maintenance:
- *Protect bean and pea seeds and soft fruits from bird attack using netting.*

- *Provide a drip-style hose irrigation system that can be controlled by a timer.*
- *Allow for hand watering by hose at planting time and for specific areas.*
- *Water evenly to maintain growth, and thoroughly to encourage deep roots.*
- *Remove weeds regularly or use an organic weed-suppressant mat.*
- *Avoid treading and compacting moist soil when planting and weeding.*
- *Lay horticultural fleece over beds of seedlings to discourage insect pests and provide protection in cold weather.*

EDIBLE BOUNTY GARDEN PLAN

cottage-style
flower garden

chicken
shed

reclaimed
wood for posts

open area for
planting up
and storage

large wooden
hot-pile
compost bins

pool

bench

veranda for
hanging baskets
and potted plants

pale gravel
beach shingle

pathway
of stepping
stones set
in gravel

Plant list

1 *Tropaeolum majus*
2 *Beta vulgaris*
3 *Daucus carota*
4 *Brassica rapa*
5 *Petroselinum crispum*
6 *Phaseolus vulgaris* var.
   nanus
7 *Ocimum sanctum*
8 *Solanum lycopersicum*
9 *Spinacia oleracea*
10 *Brassica oleracea 'Hispi'*
11 *Vicia faba*
12 *Brassica oleracea* var.
   capitata
13 *Beta vulgaris ssp cicla*
14 *Brassica rapa*
15 *Lactuca Sativa 'Lollo Rossa'*
16 *Allium schoenoprasum*
17 *Pisum sativum 'Dwarf
   Sweet Green'*

Below: *Vegetables and taller
herbs are supported with sticks
and brushwood from early on
in their growth.*

Right: *A throne-like garden
chair is positioned to look
into the spiral-shaped
vegetable plot.*

Above: *Legumes enrich the soil by converting nitrogen from the atmosphere.*

Above: *Swiss or ruby chard make the plot more decorative with their colourful stems.*

Above: *The large shed makes a rustic backdrop for this relaxed kitchen garden.*

MAKING A HOT-PILE COMPOST BIN

Every productive garden should have a compost heap where organic materials are recycled to create a highly nutritious soil conditioner. Use any vegetable matter that is disease free and will rot down.

1 Place the bin on the soil, water and add twiggy material.
2 Add alternating bands of drier 'brown' materials and fresher 'greens'. This introduces oxygen and prevents the pile from becoming wet and airless.
3 Every couple of layers add decomposing microbes with compost from another heap, or garden soil. Leaves of nettle or comfrey act as activators.
4 Cover the bin to conserve heat and moisture.

Nitrogen-rich 'greens' include grass cuttings, raw fruit and vegetables, seaweed and garden pond clearings, tea leaves, manure, non-seeding annual weeds and soft hedge clippings.
Carbon-rich 'browns' include coffee grounds, dry plant stems and twigs (preferably shredded), scrunched-up paper, egg shells, straw, hay and torn-up cardboard. Water the brown layers in the bin.

HOT-PILE COMPOST BIN CROSS-SECTION

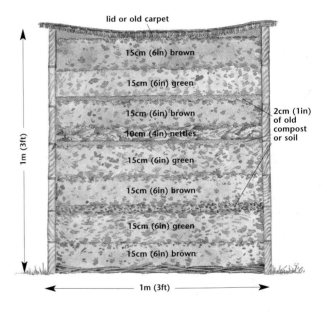

lid or old carpet

15cm (6in) brown
15cm (6in) green
15cm (6in) brown
10cm (4in) nettles
15cm (6in) green
15cm (6in) brown
15cm (6in) green
15cm (6in) brown

2cm (1in) of old compost or soil

1m (3ft)

1m (3ft)

SETTING PAVING SLABS IN GRAVEL

Gravel is a relatively low-cost alternative to paving, but in large areas it can feel monotonous. Add textural variety with paving slabs as shown below, or use real or concrete wood-effect sleepers. Another advantage in introducing paving slabs or sleepers into an area of gravel is that they provide a more secure passage for foot traffic.

1 Lay out the tiles or paving slabs. The ones used here are sandstone pavers with a riven surface, but you could use quarry tiles or concrete, stone-effect paving.

2 Ease away the gravel around a tile to mark where to dig. Remove the tile and excavate a square hole, just large enough to accommodate it, scooping out the hardcore.

3 Set the tile back in the hole and check it is at the same level as the gravel. Move the gravel back around the tile using a straight-edged piece of wood to level it out.

4 Quarry tiles or small slabs can relieve large uniform areas of gravel or slate. Set them closer together to form a grid to create a level sitting area.

CALM OASIS

A thoughtful approach to balance and harmony in this enclosed city garden has resulted in a restorative haven that stimulates the senses. The garden design interprets the opposing forces of yin and yang, while reflecting four of the basic elements – metal, fire, earth and water – in the materials used in its construction and in the colours of the planting.

Above: *The Buddha statue provides a calming aid to focus meditation.*

A high terrace leading from the house provides a west-facing platform from which to view the overall scene, with a black metal table and chairs positioned on the paving where they can take full

Above: Cordyline australis *loves full sun; the spiky foliage provides a sense of energy and optimism.*

advantage of the summer sunsets. Steps descend to a slate path that divides the energetic, south-facing, yang side of the garden, with its hot and fiery planting, from the cool yin subjects that languish quietly on the opposite side of the path. The resulting effect is one of calm tranquillity and quiet harmony.

The path, which turns at right angles to create an indirect route through the garden, leads to a quiet pool traversed by stepping-stones. The pool is watched over by a contemplative Buddha, who sits calmly in front of a narrow mirror that rests informally against a wall.

The meandering journey taken by the path keeps visitors guessing at what will be around the next corner, thus giving the garden an element of mystery and surprise. A thick screen of rustling bamboo obscures the bottom of the garden completely from view.

The path eventually culminates in a secret woodland glade where there is a reward waiting for anybody making the journey – a bamboo deckchair in which to rest, relax and meditate.

Dividing a garden into clearly defined sections, like this one, is an excellent way of disguising a long, narrow plot. The eye takes in only one discrete area after another, rather than seeing the whole garden in a single glance.

The garden plan for this Calm Oasis courtyard, shown overleaf, shows the visual dynamics of the space, and also includes practical sequences on making a slate path and planting an ornamental water plant in a pond, both features that are included here.

Right: *The generously proportioned raised terrace offers a delightful vista over the luxuriant planting throughout the garden.*

CREATING A CONTEMPLATIVE GARDEN

Flooring:
• *Keep hard landscaping to a minimum and use natural materials.*
• *Use curving, meandering, forms in paths and beds.*
• *Create stepping-stone paths through grass and gravel areas.*

Walls and Screens:
Create a sense of enclosure and privacy.
• *Plant the boundaries densely with tall shrubs and trees, such as bamboo or silver birch.*

• *Add screens made from willow or bamboo canes to break up areas and provide backdrops for set pieces.*

Plants and Containers:
• *Keep planting uncluttered by keeping to a small number of species.*
• *Concentrate on foliage effect, especially grasses, bamboo and other slender forms that have movement and make sounds in the breeze.*
• *Include some clipped evergreen cloud topiary for structure and form.*

Water Features:
• *Use water to achieve a calming effect, to introduce light and movement, and to encourage nature and wildlife.*
• *Features might include a gazing pool, a stream or a rill.*
• *Encourage birds with a shallow, water-filled drinking and bathing vessel.*

Structures and Ornament:
• *Create sheltered seating areas.*
• *Place symbolic sculptural statements at strategic points.*

CALM OASIS GARDEN PLAN

Buddha head

fence

brick wall

pool

stepping stones

Irish limestone flags

grey Snowdonian slate

timber edging

Plant list

1. *Equisetum hyemale*
2. *Holboellia latifolia*
3. *Euphorbia mellifera*
4. *Phormium tenax*
5. *Dodonaea viscosa* 'Purpurea'
6. *Trachycarpus fortunei*
7. *Sophora microphylla*
8. *Cordyline australis*
9. *Yucca rostrata*
10. *Albizia julibrissin* 'Rosea'
11. *Iris confusa*
12. *Yucca* sp.
13. *Astelia chathamica*
14. *Beschorneria yuccoides*
15. *Festuca glauca*
16. *Agapanthus africanus*
17. *Crocosmia* 'Solfaterre'
18. *Melianthus major*
19. *Euphorbia amygdaloides* 'Purpurea'
20. *Canna* 'Durban'
21. *Musa basjoo*
22. *Polystichum setiferum* 'Divisilobum'
23. *Phyllostachys aurea*

Right: *Irish limestone flags, used here for the raised terrace, are highly stain resistant.*

Left: *A number of cabbage palms (Cordyline australis) are positioned around the dining area in this courtyard. This plant thrives in full sun and semi-shade.*

Above: *Silver Spear (Astelia chathamica) are planted in two tall, angular stoneware urns that act as an informal entranceway to the planted areas beyond the flagstones.*

Above: *Feathery leaved* Albizia julibrissin *is a delicate small tree for a sheltered spot.*

Above: *Layers of bold architectural foliage create a sense of enclosure and privacy.*

Above: *The dramatic, silver-leaved* Astelia chathamica *is an evergreen perennial.*

LAYING A SLATE PATH

A slate path helps to create an atmospheric garden with a strong emphasis on natural harmony and organic materials. It is also satisfyingly crunchy underfoot. The dark colouring and interesting texture of slate makes a perfect foil for bamboo and other lush foliage plants and you can choose from a number of different shades and grades that will suit your purposes. Slate is more effective at preventing weed growth than gravel, due to weed seeds germinating in the surface layer, but being sharp-edged, it isn't kind to young children.

SLATE PATH CROSS-SECTION

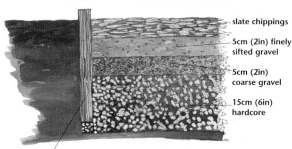

slate chippings
5cm (2in) finely sifted gravel
5cm (2in) coarse gravel
15cm (6in) hardcore

timber edging board, 30 x 2.5cm (12 x 1in)

1 Mark out the area with string and pegs and then dig out to a depth of at least 30cm (12in). Compact the surface by tamping it down thoroughly with a stout piece of timber or a garden roller.

2 Lay hardcore to a depth of 15cm (6in) and set tanalized wooden edging boards along both sides over a thin layer of hardcore, so that the boards finish at about 2.5cm (1in) above the adjacent ground. Screw the boards into stout

wooden pegs for stability. Compact the pathway with a post. The edging boards are approximately 30cm (12in) deep and 2.5cm (1in) wide.
3 Spread a layer of coarse gravel to a depth of 5cm (2in) and roll or tread all over it.

4 Cover the coarse gravel with a layer of finely sifted gravel, about 5cm (2in) deep.
5 Top with slate chippings as shown above, taking the path up to the ground surface. Soak with a hose to bind the gravel and wash away the dust.

PLANTING ORNAMENTAL HORSETAIL

The horsetail (*Equisetum hyemale*) adds an oriental flavour to a pool with its vertical, 1.2m (4ft) long stems and black banding. Miniature Cattail (*Typha minima*) would be

another good option. Use a perforated container for planting in water, as well as an aquatic compost (soil mix) and slow-release fertilizer pellets.

1 Line a perforated planting basket with hessian sacking to contain the aquatic compost (soil mix) while allowing the roots to penetrate. Pre-soak the young horsetail plants.

2 Set the plants on top of some compost so the surface is a little below the rim. Fill in between with more compost and firm. There is no need to remove perforated pots.

3 Cover the compost with washed pea gravel, to a depth of between 1.5–2cm (½–¾in). This helps to stop soil clouding the clear water and deters fish from uprooting the plants.

4 Lower the basket into the pool, resting it on stacked bricks if necessary, so the rim is just below the water surface. Try dark slate as an subtler mulch rather than pea gravel.

URBAN CHIC

This contemporary and sophisticated urban courtyard is an intimate retreat that cleverly optimizes the space within the confines imposed by a period building. Its distinctive modern feel is essentially minimalistic in concept and demonstrates an ability to cleverly reinterpret classical lines and symmetry using a range of modern materials.

Above: *Changes of level, using raised beds and steps, occur smoothly.*

In this contemporary urban courtyard, the garden room admits access to a lower terrace, which is partly enclosed by a vine-covered wall and overlooked by the home

Above: Pittosporum tobira *'Wheeler's Dwarf' is grown as a neat, small-leaved foliage plant in this raised bed.*

office – a stone-clad building with richly coloured roof tiles. Its exterior joinery is painted pale duck-egg blue, toning with the grey containers and subdued planting throughout the courtyard.

Reclaimed York-stone paving slabs make up the flooring, but a classically designed marble-tile mosaic detail has been incorporated, which creates a striking ground-level focal point in the central area. Positioned in front of glazed doors, it can be viewed from both indoors and out. The soft tile colours of cream, blue and grey pick up and reflect the tones of the other materials and finishes used in the courtyard garden.

Raised beds planted with structural evergreens, including *Pittosporum tobira* 'Nana', *Festuca glauca* and *Pittosporum tobira* 'Wheeler's Dwarf', form walls to line the steps to the upper level, which features a formal pool.

On the boundaries, brick walls surround the garden, lined on one side by black bamboo (*Phyllostachys nigra*) and on the return by a bold, oak-framed pergola. Planting throughout the courtyard is in architectural blocks following the lines of the hard landscaping, with mop-head olive trees (*Olea europaea*) in aged zinc planters providing the main focal points.

The garden plan for this urban courtyard, shown overleaf, demonstrates how the character of the space is defined by the York stone paving and the subtlety of the planting elements. Practical sequences show how to lay a mosaic tile square and how to plant an olive tree in a steel container.

Right: *The insert of pale-coloured mosaic tiles creates a dramatic visual relief in the York stone paving. The tiles have been set flush with the surrounding flooring.*

CREATING A SMALL, MODERN GARDEN

Flooring:
• *Structure the hard landscaping into simple visual statements.*
• *Organize a clear route through the garden.*
• *Use the minimum number of different hard materials for a clear visual story.*

Walls and Screens:
• *Create an enclosure with walls, screens and planting.*

Planting and Containers:
• *Choose one style, formal or exotic.*

• *Plant in single-species blocks.*
• *Include evergreen and structural material for year-round interest.*
• *Allow for seasonal planting, especially spring bulbs and summer flowers.*
• *Choose co-ordinated planting containers that have sufficient volume to support large specimens if necessary.*

Structures and Furniture:
• *Co-ordinate the colour of exterior joinery with the landscaping.*
• *Incorporate at least one vertical structure to provide scale.*

Ornament and Water Features:
• *Include a small formal pool or rill, with a fountain to introduce elements of movement and sound.*
• *Use sculptural features.*
• *Co-ordinate the materials in colour, type and texture, allowing for one or two contrast details.*
• *Focus on water and sculpture features, architectural planting and wall textures.*

Lighting:
• *Introduce lighting to bring an extra dimension to the garden at night.*

URBAN CHIC GARDEN PLAN

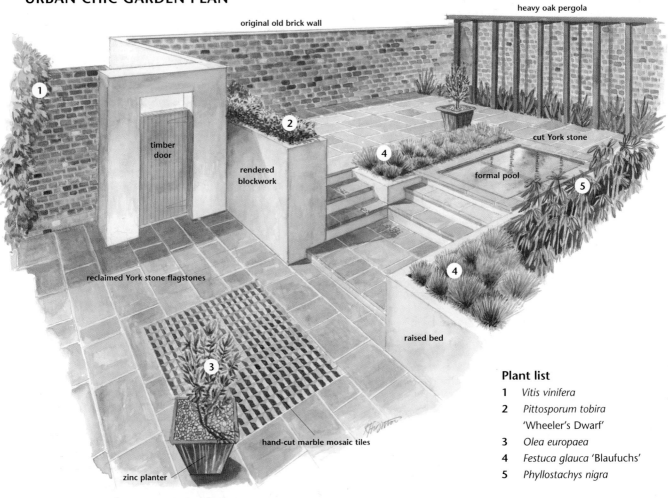

heavy oak pergola

original old brick wall

timber door

rendered blockwork

cut York stone

formal pool

1

2

4

5

4

reclaimed York stone flagstones

raised bed

3

4

hand-cut marble mosaic tiles

zinc planter

Plant list
1 *Vitis vinifera*
2 *Pittosporum tobira* 'Wheeler's Dwarf'
3 *Olea europaea*
4 *Festuca glauca* 'Blaufuchs'
5 *Phyllostachys nigra*

Left: *The formal zinc planters create elegant, understated focal points in this courtyard. See also the practical planting sequence shown opposite.*

Below: *The blue-grey foliage of Festuca glauca 'Blausilber' is used in the raised beds. The colour fits perfectly with the muted scheme.*

Above: *The mosaic tile inset creates a dramatic visual relief in the paving.*

Above: *Vitis vinifera 'Purpurea' self-clings by suckers to the side wall.*

Above: *The whole composition is unified with the use of York stone paving.*

LAYING THE MOSAIC TILE SQUARE

The York-stone paving in the courtyard opposite has been embellished by the inclusion of a square inset of geometric blue and grey tiles directly outside the house. The mosaic tile square adds attractive detailing to the hard landscaping, breaking up the expanse of pale-coloured flooring. The following method shows how to create a similar effect. The tiles of the mosaic finish flush with the York stone so that furniture can be positioned anywhere without any change in level.

MOSAIC TILE SQUARE CROSS-SECTION

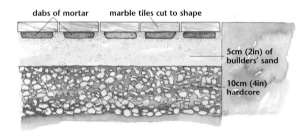

dabs of mortar   marble tiles cut to shape

5cm (2in) of builders' sand

10cm (4in) hardcore

1 Plan your design allowing for a 5mm (¼in) space between each tile for mortar. Calculate the number of tiles.
2 Mark out the area for tiling using string and pegs, making sure that the corners form exact right angles. Prepare the foundations by digging down to around 20cm (8in).
3 Add hardcore at least 10cm (4in) deep and compact with a sledgehammer or post. Spread a 5cm (2in) layer of builders' sand over the hardcore. Smooth with a rake.

4 Cut tiles to shape with an angle grinder, following safety regulations, and arrange in the desired pattern before laying.
5 Start at the centre and, working in small areas, dab mortar on the sand where each tile will lie. Position the tiles, adding a small dab to their edges. Tap down gently and check levels in both directions as you go.
6 Finish by working dark coloured mortar into the gaps, brushing surplus away before it dries.

PLANTING AN OLIVE TREE

Modern metallic containers with a weathered or satin finish work well in a minimalist urban courtyard. The look is perfected when planted with specimens that have a similarly muted colouring and simple profile. Increasingly popular and ideal for a sheltered courtyard are olive trees, with their handsome grey-green leaves.

1 Insulate the galvanized metal planter using sheets of polystyrene (Styrofoam) or bubble wrap/greenhouse insulation material. You could also pack insulation material around an inner plastic pot.

2 Cover, but do not block, the drainage hole with a crock and a layer of gravel, and add soil-based potting mix with extra grit. Having presoaked the olive tree, remove its pot and position the plant.

3 Finish off by adding a layer of mulch comprising fine-grade decorative golden gravel, slate chippings or coloured acrylic chips or beads.

4 Stand the planter in a sheltered spot, such as against a warm wall. In winter, water the olive tree sparingly and in prolonged cold and wet spells bring it under cover somewhere frost free.

PLANTING CHOICES

Plants are the raison d'être of a patio or courtyard garden. They can shape the design, create different moods and change through the seasons to provide constant interest. This directory does not set out to be exhaustive, but is instead designed to help you select some of the best plants for your style of patio. It focuses on all the important aspects of furnishing your outdoor room year round with leaves and flowers, including examples of architectural and dramatic specimens, heat- and shade-tolerant plants, ones suitable for container cultivation and ones for covering walls and trellis partitions. Though patios are often relatively small, a single specimen tree can transform the look and feel of the space, creating shade and an overhead canopy of branches, so enhancing the room-like quality. A range of evergreens gives a continuity of display, providing a backdrop to the ebb and flow of seasonal plants.

Left: *A cottage garden style display like this looks wonderful in summer, but for colour and interest throughout the year mix in evergreens and plants that bloom in other seasons.*

TREES FOR SMALL SPACES

Good planting design depends on a strong framework, and, even in a confined space, trees are an essential part of the plan. When choosing a deciduous tree, pick one that will develop a striking winter profile, especially one with ornamental or edible fruits, flowers, coloured or handsomely shaped leaves and attractive bark. Some large trees make excellent hedging and green architecture.

Above: Crataegus laevigata *'Paul's Scarlet'* *is an easy tree for city and country gardens.*

Catalpa bignonioides 'Aurea'
Golden Indian bean tree

This luminous form of the Indian bean tree is ideal for adding an exotic touch to a sheltered courtyard or terrace. With its light canopy of broad, lime green, heart-shaped leaves, it creates a strong focal point in a garden right through summer and into autumn (fall).
Height and spread: 10 x 10m (33 x 33ft); much less if pruned
Hardiness: Hardy/Z 6–10
Cultivation: Prune this deciduous tree back hard every other year in spring to control its size and encourage the formation of even larger, more richly coloured leaves.

Cercis canadensis 'Forest Pansy'
Eastern redbud

A deciduous tree grown mainly for its heart-shaped leaves – which are a rich plum-purple in this cultivar – but also for its ability to form a graceful outline as it grows to maturity. The leaves turn yellow in autumn (fall) before falling.

Height and spread: To 10 x 10m (33 x 33ft)
Hardiness: Hardy/Z 5–9
Cultivation: Grow in fertile, well-drained soil in sun or light shade. Stake young trees for the first three years. Established trees may be cut back hard in spring to encourage larger leaves.

Cercis siliquastrum
Judas tree

This Mediterranean species thrives in a sunny courtyard, perhaps growing with the benefit of the shelter offered by a wall. The small and beautifully formed leaves are rounded with notched ends, and the curious clusters of purple-pink blossoms, which often arise directly from the bark of more established branches, show in spring either before or during the emergence of the leaves.
Height and spread: Eventually up to 10 x 10m (33 x 33ft)
Hardiness: Hardy/Z 7
Cultivation: Plant in well-drained loam, improved before planting if poor, in a warm, sunny or lightly shaded spot.

Cornus
Dogwood

Several of these slow-growing North American trees, including *Cornus kousa* var. *chinensis*, whose bracts fade to pink, the free-flowering 'China Girl' and conical 'Eddie's White Wonder', are noted for their suitability in confined spaces and long season of interest. As well as the showy 'flowers' there may be ornamental fruits and autumn (fall) leaf colour. In *C. alternifolia* 'Argentea' and the larger growing pagoda tree, *Cornus contraversa*, branches develop in a series of horizontal whorls or tiers. The cream variegated *C. c.* 'Variegata' is slow to establish and grow initially but worth the wait!
Height and spread: *Cornus kousa* 7 x 5m (23 x 16ft); *C.* 'Eddie's White Wonder' 6 x 5m (20 x 16ft); *C. contraversa* 'Variegata' 3–5 x 3m (10–16 x 10ft), and 8 x 8m (25 x 25ft) ultimately
Hardiness: Hardy/Z 5–8
Cultivation: Neutral to acid, humus-rich soil in sun or light shade and sheltered from wind.

Crataegus laevigata 'Paul's Scarlet'
Midland hawthorn

In late spring, clusters of rich carmine pink double blossoms smother this thorny deciduous tree. Although ideal for more relaxed, cottage garden planting, this is also a good specimen for cities, being tolerant of atmospheric pollution.
Height and spread: 6–8 x 5m (20–25 x 16ft)
Hardiness: Hardy/Z 4–7
Cultivation: Most soils will do but avoid waterlogged conditions.

Cupressus sempervirens Stricta Group
Italian cypress

These slender columns bring to mind sun-scorched slopes of Mediterranean hillsides and the formal gardens of the Italian Renaissance. A single plant adds just the right character to a terracotta-filled courtyard, but in larger terraces you can create striking vistas by planting in rows and avenues. On a smaller scale, try the hardy columnar juniper *Juniperus scopulorum*

Above: C. bignonioides *'Aurea'*

Above: Cercis siliquastrum

Above: Cornus kousa

Above: Cupressus sempervirens

Above: Olea europaea

Above: Magnolia x loebneri

'Blue Arrow' – a superior selection replacing the aptly named 'Skyrocket'.

Height and spread: 20 x 3m (70 x 10ft) at maturity; 'Blue Arrow' 6m x 50–60cm (20ft x 20–24in)

Hardiness: *C. sempervirens* hardy/Z 7–9; *J.* 'Blue Arrow' hardy/Z 3–7

Cultivation: Plant Italian cypress on free-draining ground. Water to establish, especially in poor dry soils, but avoid excess watering as this can cause the normally upright branches to splay out, spoiling the profile. Dislikes cold winds.

Fagus sylvatica
Beech
Along with hornbeam (*Carpinus*), beech can be clipped into large architectural elements within a formal courtyard, including boundary hedges, dividing walls and archways. Although deciduous, plants hang on to their dried coppery leaves through winter, providing a colourful backdrop for glossy evergreens. A good hedge for colder, more exposed gardens and cottage-style plantings. The copper beech, *F. s.* f. *purpurea*, has deep purple leaves.

Height and spread: As a hedge, beech is most often clipped to 1.2–3m (4–10ft) in height and up to 1m (3ft) wide

Hardiness: Hardy/Z 4–7

Cultivation: Any well-drained soil tolerating lime, in sun or light shade.

Magnolia x loebneri 'Leonard Messel'
Magnolia
A beautiful rounded tree, this variety produces pale lilac-pink blooms with relatively narrow petals in mid-spring. The contrasting effect of the pale flowers against the darker buds and bare branches is enchanting. The more upright 'Merrill' has white flowers.

Height and spread: 5–6 x 5–6m (16–20 x 16–20ft)

Hardiness: Hardy/Z 5–7

Cultivation: Grow on well-drained but humus-rich soil, ideally neutral to acid though some lime is tolerated. Sun or light shade.

Malus 'Evereste'
Crab apple
Though there are many varieties to choose from with late spring blossom, colourful autumn (fall) fruits and good autumn colour, 'Evereste' stands out as a fine example. This conical tree has fragrant white blossoms, which contrast with the red buds in late spring and an autumn crop of orange-yellow crab apples that develop red where they catch the sun. 'Red Sentinel' is similar to 'Evereste' but with dark red fruits.

Height and spread: 7 x 6m (23 x 20ft)

Hardiness: Hardy/Z 4–9

Cultivation: Grow on any well-drained but not dry soil in sun or light shade.

Above: Malus *'Evereste'*

Olea europaea
Olive
The European olive is gaining in popularity as a garden plant, though it is unlikely to fruit in cold climates. It naturally assumes a pleasing shape – usually dome-headed – and the narrow grey-green leaves are attractive. An olive is ideal for a container and makes a fine feature in a Mediterranean planting scheme. In frost-prone areas, some winter protection is necessary.

Height and spread: To 10 x 10m (33 x 33ft), but usually much less in cultivation

Hardiness: Borderline hardy/Z 8

Cultivation: Grow in fertile, well-drained soil in full sun.

Prunus
Ornamental cherry
This huge genus includes some of the best-loved spring-flowering trees. 'Snow Goose' has white flowers and 'Okame' shocking pink. *P. mume* 'Beni-shidori' (Japanese apricot) with deep pink flowers is ideal for wall training. A form of Yoshino cherry, *P. x yedoensis* 'Ivensii' has horizontal branches, white flowers and pink buds.
P. 'Amanogawa' makes a pillar clothed in semi-double, shell pink flowers in late spring.
P. 'Spire' is similar with good autumn (fall) colour. *Prunus subhirtella* 'Autumnalis Rosea' produces a light tracery of branches clothed from autumn until spring with sprigs of pale pink blossom.

Height and spread:
P. 'Amanogawa' around 8 x 4m (25 x 13ft); *P.* 'Spire' around 8 x 7m (25 x 23ft)

Hardiness: Hardy/Z 6–9

Cultivation: Grow in any moderately fertile soil in full sun; a little lime seems to suit the trees.

CLIMBERS AND WALL SHRUBS

This plant group is essential in a courtyard, where the boundaries and dividing screens play such a significant role in defining the space. With an appropriate balance of evergreens, flowering shrubs and ornamental vines, it is possible to swathe the walls and overhead structures of the courtyard with colour and texture that will last throughout the year.

Above: Abutilon megapotamicum *flowers look like Chinese paper lanterns.*

Abutilon
Flowering maple

These evergreen to deciduous flowering shrubs prefer the shelter of a warm wall unless grown in frost-free conditions. The wiry, lax stems of *A. megapotamicum*, with scarlet red and yellow bicoloured pendant blooms, or the cultivar 'Kentish Belle', which has apricot flowers, are best tied into horizontal wire supports. They flower through summer into autumn (fall). More tree-like are the earlier flowering cultivars of the hybrid *A. x suntense*, which have larger, dish-shaped blooms in shades of purple or white, together with *A. vitifolium*, the white form *A. v.* var. *album* and mauve 'Veronica Tennant'.

Height and spread: *A. megapotamicum* and *A.* 'Kentish Belle' 2–2.5 x 2–2.5m (6–8 x 6–8ft); *A. x suntense* 4 x 2.5m (13 x 8ft)

Hardiness: Frost hardy/Z 8–9

Cultivation: Grow in full sun, shelter and well-drained soil. Protect from frost with fleece.

Campsis radicans
Trumpet vine or creeper

Seldom seen in northern gardens, the orange-red, trumpet-like flowers of this vigorous, deciduous climber make an impressive show from late summer to autumn (fall) amid the profusion of pinnate leaves. The hybrid *C. x tagliabuana* 'Madame Galen' has larger blooms.

Height and spread: To 10 x 10m (33 x 33ft)

Hardiness: Borderline hardy/Z 5–9

Cultivation: Grow in any fertile, well-drained soil in full sun. Provide initial support with wires on walls.

Ceanothus
California lilac

Few wall shrubs match the impact of these fast-growing shrubs when they are smothered with their small but densely clustered distinctive fluffy blue flowers. Colours range from pale powder blue to glowing indigo. There are both deciduous and evergreen forms, the evergreens being slightly less hardy and thus a riskier choice in a cold district, though neither form is long-lived. They flower either in late spring to early summer or in late summer. Spring-flowering evergreens include 'Delight', 'Italian Skies' and 'Puget Blue', all with rich blue flowers.

Height and spread: To 2 x 2m (6 x 6ft), or sometimes more

Hardiness: Borderline hardy/Z 7–9

Cultivation: Grow in any fertile, well-drained soil in full sun. Prune after flowering, if necessary, but avoid hard pruning.

Chaenomeles
Ornamental quince, japonica

It is possible to train these somewhat intractable, thorny plants tight against a wall, but it is easier to tie them loosely to it and allow the stems to billow forward more informally. The cup-shaped flowers, which appear either before or at the same time as the leaves unfurl in spring, are charming. *C. speciosa* 'Geisha Girl' has apricot flowers and a neater habit than most. The hybrid group *C. x superba* includes a number of worthwhile selections

Above: Ceanothus

Above: Chaenomeles japonica

Above: Campsis radicans

Above: Clematis montana

Above: Clematis alpina

Above: Fremontodendron

in red, white and pink. Among the reds, 'Knap Hill Scarlet', with its large, bright red flowers, is perhaps one of the best. 'Crimson and Gold' has the added attraction of vivid yellow stamens, which contrast with the flowers. The small greenish yellow aromatic fruits, rich in pectin, may be used for jelly.
Height and spread: 1.5 x 1.5m (5 x 5ft)
Hardiness: Hardy/Z 5–9
Cultivation: Grow in fertile, well-drained soil in sun or light shade (north walls tolerated). Survives in most soils other than lime-rich or waterlogged ones.

Clematis
Clematis

It is possible to have a species or hybrid in flower during virtually every season of the year. Best known are the early and late summer-flowering hybrids. The showiest have large, flat blooms, plain or striped and often in strong, rich

colours, like the carmine 'Rouge Cardinal'. 'Marie Boisselot', is an excellent white. One of the best of the blues with a profusion of medium-sized blooms is 'Perle d'Azur', which flowers for weeks through summer into autumn (fall). For containers, try some of the new compact-growing large-flowered varieties like the double white 'Arctic Queen'. If you are nervous about pruning, forms of the later summer-flowering *C. viticella* group are easy and productive, and the bell-shaped blooms of *C. texensis* hybrids such as 'Gravetye Beauty' provide sumptuous displays.

The species have daintier flowers, though some are rampant growers. This makes them suitable for screening a large area (although only *C. armandii* is evergreen). The early spring-flowering *C. alpina* is elegant, with its nodding, bell-like flowers and ferny foliage. Selections are available

in blue, pink and white. *C. macropetala* is similar, with several pretty 'cottage garden' forms such as the double 'Markham's Pink'. The Mediterranean-looking evergreen, *C. armandii*, has long leathery leaves, and fragrant white flowers in spring. Also scented, especially 'Elizabeth', are selections of the rampant May-flowering *C. montana*, which will usefully adapt to a north wall or fence. Also shade tolerant but flowering later are the ferny leaved *C. tangutica* and *C.* 'Bill Mackenzie', with yellow, citrus peel, lantern-like flowers in late summer to autumn and silky whorled ornamental seed heads.
Height and spread: To 10 x 10m (33 x 33ft) (most species); to 3 x 3m (10 x 10ft) (hybrids and smaller species like *C. alpina*)
Hardiness: Hardy/Z 4–9
Cultivation: Grow in most fertile, well-drained soils, preferably alkaline. Site in sun or (ideally) partial shade, making sure the roots are in shade. Pruning requirements vary with the different types, and you should refer to a specialist guide for details, but many late summer-flowering kinds (in pruning group 3), including *C. viticella* and *C.* 'Perle d'Azur', are easily dealt with: cut them to 30cm (12in) from ground level in late winter.

Eccremocarpus scaber
Chilean glory vine

This climber is often grown from seed as an annual, but can behave as a perennial, producing feathery foliage each year and bright orange tubular flowers until well into autumn (fall). Effective when allowed to scramble freely through an evergreen hedge or shrub.
Height and spread: 3 x 1m (10 x 3ft)
Hardiness: Borderline hardy/ Z 9–10
Cultivation: Grow in well-drained soil in sun, protecting the underground tubers in cold regions with a deep insulating mulch. Suitable for containers.

Fremontodendron
'California Glory'
Fremontia, flannelbush

The form 'California Glory' is a vigorous sub-tropical-looking wall shrub that can climb the façade of a house. It produces its large, saucer-shaped waxy yellow blooms from late spring to early autumn (fall). The dark green lobed leaves make a fine contrast but beware the rusty coloured bristle hairs, which can irritate skin.
Height and spread: 6 x 4m (20 x 13ft)
Hardiness: Frost hardy/Z 9–10
Cultivation: Any well-drained neutral to alkaline soil with sun and shelter. Cut off outward-facing shoots and tie onto wire supports.

Above: Humulus lupulus *'Aureus'*

Above: Hydrangea anomala

Above: P. quinquefolia

Hedera
Ivy
The ivies, all self-clinging, will bring green to even the most inhospitable parts of a terrace or courtyard, and there is more variety in leaf shape and colour than you might imagine. *H. canariensis* is a large-leaved species from the Canary Isles, usually grown in one of its variegated forms such as 'Gloire de Marengo', whose green leaves are irregularly margined with cream (deepening to yellow as they mature). It needs a fairly sheltered spot. For tougher locations, grow the similar looking *H. colchica* 'Dentata Variegata' or yellow-centred 'Sulphur Heart'. The smaller-leaved *H. helix* is tougher, in fact virtually indestructible: 'Glacier' has creamy edged grey-green leaves; 'Green Ripple' is vigorous, with distinctive, frilly-edged leaves and 'Buttercup' is slow growing and lime green.

Height and spread: *H. canariensis* 'Gloire de Marengo' to 4 x 4m (13 x 13ft); *H. helix* cultivars to 45cm–8m x 45cm–8m (18in–25ft x 18in–25ft)
Hardiness: *H. canariensis* 'Gloire de Marengo' borderline hardy/Z 8–9; *H. helix* cultivars hardy/Z 5
Cultivation: Grow in almost any soil. Variegated forms need some sun for the best leaf colour, while plain-leaved varieties do well even in deep shade.

Humulus lupulus 'Aureus'
Golden hop
This herbaceous twining climber is a prodigious grower. Once established, it will cover a wall or a pergola each year, making it useful for a seasonal curtain of foliage. Don't try to train it, apart from in its initial stages – just let the stems loosely support the yellow-green leaves. Clusters of hops form in later summer. The bristly stems and leaves may irritate sensitive skin, so wear gloves when cutting back.
Height and spread: To 6 x 6m (20 x 20ft)
Hardiness: Hardy/Z 6–9
Cultivation: Grow in reasonably fertile, well-drained soil, in sun for the brightest leaf colour, though it also does well in shade. Avoid dry, windy conditions.

Hydrangea anomala subsp. *petiolaris*
Climbing hydrangea
The most commonly grown of the climbing hydrangeas is a useful plant for covering a north-facing or shady wall. These woodland plants cling to walls and fences via adventitious roots. The bright green heart-shaped leaves form a dense covering and foil for the creamy white frothy flower heads in autumn (fall). Butter yellow autumn foliage.
Height and spread: 15 x 15m (50 x 50ft)
Hardiness: Hardy/Z 5–8
Cultivation: Provide initial support for shoots of young plants to keep them in contact with the wall.

Parthenocissus spp.
Virginia creeper
These foliage plants are grown for their autumn (fall) colour and are ideal for covering large walls or for forming curtains over the sides of high retaining walls or pergolas. *P. henryana* has dark green leaves veined and shaded with silver, turning red in autumn and is especially useful for north-facing aspects. Its spread is easily controlled by cutting back. *P. tricuspidata* is the well-known Boston ivy, and *P. quinquefolia* the Virginia creeper. Both are suitable only for larger gardens or for growing up into mature trees. *P. t.* 'Veitchii' has leaves that open purple in spring, mature to green, then turn red-purple in autumn given a sunny spot.
Height and spread: *P. henryana* 10 x 10m (33 x 33ft); *P. tricuspidata* 20m (65ft)
Hardiness: Hardy/Z 4–9; *P. henryana* borderline hardy/Z 7–9
Cultivation: Grow in fertile, well-drained soil in sun or partial shade.

Rosa
Rose
Few flowers can match the rose for pure, old-fashioned charm, and the modern repeat-flowering climbing forms are useful where space is limited. The following are all tried and tested. 'Madame Alfred Carrière', with an abundance of rather untidy but sweetly scented creamy white flowers in summer, is especially versatile, lighting up a wall, clambering through a mature tree or swathing a sturdy pergola or arch.

Above: Rosa *'Gloire de Dijon'*

'Félicité Perpétue' has dainty, crumpled flowers that open pink and fade to blush white. 'Gloire de Dijon' is early flowering and needs the shelter of a warm wall in frost-prone districts; it has large, bun-like, creamy apricot blooms. 'Constance Spry' has full, double, rich pink flowers. The repeat-flowering 'The New Dawn' tolerates shade and has blush pink perfectly formed blooms and healthy, glossy foliage. 'Compassion' is similarly long flowered with apricot-tinted blooms and a delicious scent.

Height and spread: Modern repeat-flowering climbers like 'Compassion' 3 x 2.5m (10 x 8ft). Others can be to 5 x 5m (16 x 16ft) or more, depending on the variety

Hardiness: Hardy/Z 4–9

Cultivation: Grow in very fertile, well-drained soil in sun or light shade.

Solanum
Potato vine

Preferring a sheltered spot, the semi-evergreen *Solanum jasminoides* 'Album' is a beauty with an airy habit and starry white flowers, each with a yellow 'beak'. The season extends over a long period through summer into autumn (fall). Similarly prolific but hardier is the Chilean potato tree *S. crispum* 'Glasnevin' with rich purple blooms. Tie the thin stems to their support.

Above: Rosa *'Constance Spry'*

Height and spread: 3 x 3m (10 x 10ft)

Hardiness: Half hardy to frost hardy/ Z 8–11

Cultivation: Grow in any well-drained soil in full sun. In cold areas, protect with a dry mulch over winter.

Thunbergia alata
Black-eyed Susan

This striking plant, which is usually grown as an annual in cold areas, is a climber that is also effectively grown in hanging baskets and allowed to trail down. The simple yellow or orange flowers have pronounced deep purple-brown throats – resulting in the highly descriptive common name, Black-eyed Susan.

Height and spread: 2m x 25cm (6ft x 10in); spreads more where it is grown as a perennial

Hardiness: Tender/Z 10

Cultivation: It will tolerate most soils in sun or light shade.

Wisteria
Wisteria

Mature specimens of wisteria are a sight to behold in late spring, when the fragrant, pendulous flowers first emerge. Wisterias usually flower best in full sun, at least in cold climates. The plant is hardy, but the wood needs a good roasting from the sunshine to ensure flower production, hence the value of pinning the main stems to a sunny wall. In late summer, cut back any wayward growth and trim again in late winter. Garden plants are usually selections of either *W. floribunda*, the Japanese wisteria (found in violet, white or purple forms) or its similar but more vigorous cousin, *W. sinensis*, the Chinese wisteria.

Height and spread: To 9 x 9m (29 x 29ft)

Hardiness: Hardy/Z 4–10

Cultivation: Grow in any well-drained but moisture-retentive soil, preferably not too rich, in sun or light dappled shade.

Above: Wisteria

Above: Thunbergia alata

BAMBOOS, GRASSES AND GRASS-LIKE PLANTS

Grasses and their look-alikes are very much plants of the moment. Their overall form ranges from low tussocks to tall, upright columns and the linear leaves make a satisfying contrast with broad-bladed specimens. Evergreens provide forms and colours suitable for Mediterranean, oriental or contemporary courtyards.

Above: Carex morrowii *'Variegata' works well in a Japanese or contemporary setting.*

Anemanthele lessoniana
Pheasant's tail grass
Formerly listed as *Stipa arundinacea*, this colourful evergreen grass has ribbon-like arching leaves forming substantial tussocks. Orange-brown tints develop during summer, intensifying through autumn (fall). With the long-lasting drooping panicles of purple-green flower spikes, this is certainly a grass for all seasons.
Height and spread: 90 x 120cm (3 x 4ft)
Hardiness: Frost hardy/Z 7–10

Cultivation: Tidy up in early spring by removing dead material and old flower stems. Grows on well-drained to heavier clay soils in sun or light shade. Suitable for containers.

Arundo donax var. *versicolor*
Variegated Giant Reed
The species is a statuesque, bamboo-like grass often seen around coastal Mediterranean regions, thriving in damp conditions and spreading to form thickets. The white

variegated *Arundo donax* var. *versicolor* is especially showy and makes an impressive pot specimen for the summer terrace.
Height and spread: 2m x 60cm (6 x 2ft)
Hardiness: Half hardy/Z 8–10
Cultivation: Grow in sun with a plentiful supply of moisture. Cut back stems to ground level in spring.

Calamagrostis x acutiflora
Feather reed grass
This upright grass with long-lasting flower stems works effectively in groups and also when interplanted with broad-leaved perennials. 'Karl Foerster' has pinky-brown summer flowers that fade as autumn (fall) approaches and remain through the winter. 'Overdam' has the added attraction of pale yellow leaf margins.
Height and spread: 'Overdam' 1.2m x 60cm (4 x 2ft); 'Karl Foerster' 1.8m x 60cm (6ft x 2ft)

Hardiness: Hardy/Z 4–9
Cultivation: Cut down papery winter stems to ground level just as growth resumes. Best on moisture-retentive soil, rich in organic matter, in sun or part shade.

Carex
Ornamental sedge
These mostly evergreen grass-like plants offer many ornamental species and varieties, including the bronze-tinted group from New Zealand and the variegated Japanese sedges. Bronze carex include the low, arching *C. comans* forms, more upright *C. flagellifera* and varieties and the olive-coloured *C. testacea*, which includes the orange- and amber-tinted 'Prairie Fire'. The strongly upright *C. buchananii*, or leatherleaf sedge, has red-brown wiry foliage forming an upright fountain and works well in sheltered gardens or as a pot specimen, being somewhat tender. 'Frosted Curls' is pale green. Variegated *carex*, ideal for

Above: Arundo donax *var.* versicolor

Above: Calamagrostis x acutiflora *'Overdam'*

Above: Anemanthele lessoniana

Above: Deschampsia cespitosa

Above: Festuca glauca

Above: Fargesia nitida
'Nymphenburg'

lightening shaded spots, are *C. hachijoensis* 'Evergold', with low, arching tussocks of narrow, yellow-striped leaves; *C. morrowii* 'Fisher's Form', with cream-striped leaves, the diminutive *C. conica* 'Snowline', with white-edged leaves and the broad leaved, deciduous, moisture-loving *C. siderosticha* 'Variegata'.
Height and spread: 30–60cm (12–24in) x 35–45cm (14–18in)
Hardiness: Mostly frost hardy to borderline hardy except 'Evergold', which is hardy/Z 6–9.
Cultivation: Grow the bronze- and silver-leaved sedges listed on any free-draining but not dry ground and the variegated sedges on moisture-retentive soil with the exception of the moisture-loving *C. siderosticha*. You can cut bronze carex to near ground level in spring to encourage more brightly coloured regrowth; alternatively, just remove the long flowering shoots. Tidy any winter-scorched foliage on variegated forms in spring.

Deschampsia cespitosa
Tufted hair grass
This versatile grass makes an evergreen tussock of narrow, deep green leaves. In summer these produce tall, airy, arching panicles that will catch even the lightest of breezes. The flowers of the different cultivars (among them 'Bronzeschleier', *D. c.* var. *vivipara* and 'Goldschleier') eventually fade to pale biscuit by autumn (fall), providing a gossamer foil for late-flowering perennials.
Height and spread: 1.2 x 1.2m (4 x 4ft)
Hardiness: Hardy/Z 3–7
Cultivation: Grow on any neutral to acid free-draining to damp soil, incorporating plenty of organic matter at planting time. Best in sun or light shade. Excellent container specimen. Tidy plants in spring before new shoots appear.

Fargesia
Two dainty-leaved columnar to arching bamboos suitable for container gardening or smaller courtyards include the umbrella bamboo, *Fargesia murieliae*, which is sun and wind tolerant, and its forms, together with the shade-loving *F. nitida*, whose dark purple canes do not produce leaf whorls until their second year. *F. murieliae* 'Simba' is compact growing and ideal for large pots on the terrace.
Height and spread: *F. murieliae* 'Simba' 1.8m x 60cm (6 x 2ft); *F. nitida* 5 x 1.5–1.8m (16 x 5–6ft). Growth is less in containers.
Hardiness: Hardy/Z 6–11
Cultivation: Grow in moisture-retentive ground in sun or light shade. *F. nitida* needs wind shelter and dappled shade. Control spread by pruning (see pages 242–3).

Festuca glauca
Blue fescue
These tufty grasses, steely blue in colour, have a variety of uses. Grow them as a low border edging, in groups or to fill a pot. Look for varieties such as 'Harz', 'Elijah Blue' or 'Blaufuchs', which have strongly coloured leaves. The summer flowers are an added bonus but can be removed when they turn to biscuit as this can mar the display.
Height and spread: 30 x 30cm (12 x 12in)
Hardiness: Hardy/Z 4–8
Cultivation: Grow in any well-drained soil, preferably in sun. Tidy plants in spring by combing through with fingers to remove dead material.

Hakonechloa macra 'Aureola'
Japanese hakone grass
This yellow-striped *Hakonechloa* is a hardy deciduous grass with soft tapering leaves that arch to form a mound. Excellent as a pot specimen, it works well blocked in informal groups and mixed with other plants such as blue hostas and ferns for an oriental touch. Late summer and autumn (fall) tints are reddish, and airy flowers remain until late in the season.
Height and spread: 25–35 x 40–90cm (10–14 x 16–36in)
Hardiness: Hardy/Z 5–9
Cultivation: Grow on moisture-retentive but free-draining, neutral to lime-free loam or loam-based compost (soil mix) for containers. Tidy plants in spring by removing the dead foliage. Light shade prevents scorching.

Above: Miscanthus sinensis *'Zebrinus'*

Imperata cylindrica
'Rubra' syn. 'Red Baron'
Japanese blood grass

The deep crimson red-shaded leaves of this slowly creeping perennial grass are the main attraction. Grow it where it won't be overshadowed by other plants in the border or give it pride of place in a container. Plants can take a while to get going in a cold spring, and cosseting young plants pays dividends.

Height and spread: 40 x 40cm (16 x 16in)

Hardiness: Frost hardy/Z 5–9

Cultivation: Provide an insulating mulch through winter to protect roots from frost. Grow in moisture-retentive, humus-rich soil in sun or light shade.

Libertia peregrinans
New Zealand iris

Though not really a grass, this evergreen perennial is a look-alike with tufts of stiff, narrow leaves. These are amber-tinted and especially attractive when the light shines through them. New on the scene, 'Taupo Sunset' and 'Taupo Blaze' are even more brightly coloured and the foliage makes a fine foil for the small white blooms that appear on upright stems in spring and summer, before becoming orange seed heads.

Height and spread:
L. peregrinans 38 x 70cm (15 x 28in); 'Taupo Sunset' 60 x 70cm (24 x 28in)

Hardiness: Frost hardy/Z 7–9

Cultivation: Grow *L. peregrinans* in a warm, sheltered spot in full sun or light shade. Drought tolerant. Mulch in cold regions to protect roots in winter. 'Taupo Sunset' prefers more moisture.

Miscanthus sinensis
Eulalia

These elegant grasses, which range from tall, back of the border specimens to compact 'dwarfs', make arching clumps or upright columns of leaves topped by plumes of silvery, pinkish or brownish flowers that give a fountain effect in the courtyard. The selection 'Gracillimus', sometimes referred to as maiden grass, is especially fine, with slender leaves marked with a white midrib that curl pleasingly at the tips. 'Morning Light' is similar but slightly taller with a narrow white margin. 'Silberfeder' is tall with especially striking flower heads, but for small spaces try 'Kleine Silberspinne'. Of different character altogether is 'Zebrinus', with ribbon-like leaves, banded horizontally with yellow.

Height and spread: 'Gracillimus' 1.3–1.5 x 1.2m (4½–5ft x 4ft); 'Silberfeder' 1.8 x 1.2m (6 x 4ft); 'Kleine Silbespinne' 1.2m (4ft)

Hardiness: Hardy/Z 5–10

Cultivation: Grow in sun or light shade in any soil that does not become waterlogged or very dry.

Ophiopogon planiscapus
'Nigrescens'
Black mondo grass

This diminutive plant is not actually a grass, though it looks very much like one with its firm, strap-like leaves. The colour is the main point of interest – the closest there is in the plant world to a true black. It looks good in a gravel garden or against white marble chippings, which provide a contrast, and is both drought and shade tolerant. It slowly produces a carpet of black tussocks. The plain green *O. planiscapus* is a similarly tolerant and versatile ground cover plant.

Height and spread: 20 x 20cm (8 x 8in)

Hardiness: Hardy/Z 6

Cultivation: Grow in fertile soil, preferably lime-free or slightly acid, in sun or light shade.

Panicum virgatum
Switch grass

This prairie native has glowing autumn (fall) colour and long-lasting, airy seed heads forming a cloud-like effect above the foliage. Cultivars have glaucous or red-tinged foliage, colours often being reflected in the names, such as 'Dallas Blues', 'Heavy Metal' and 'Rotstrahlbusch', and usually offer the bonus of rich plum or crimson autumn tints

Height and spread: 1–2.5 x 1m (3–8 x 3ft)

Hardiness: Hardy/Z 4–9

Cultivation: Grows in most reasonably fertile and drained soils in sun or light shade. Cut back hard in spring.

Pennisetum
Fountain grass

Though not the hardiest of ornamental grasses, these graceful tussocks, with their arching, soft, bottlebrush heads, are much sought after.

Above: O.p. 'Nigrescens'

Above: Panicum virgatum

P. alopecuroides and the compact, earlier-flowering 'Hameln' are good performers in a sheltered courtyard, cascading over paved areas or making a fountain effect in a tall container. Purple- and burgundy-shaded forms of *P. setaceum*, such as 'Burgundy Giant', are eye-catching but harder to overwinter in cool climates.

Height and spread: 60cm–1.5m x 60cm–1.2m (2–5 x 2–4ft)

Hardiness: Frost hardy/Z 5–9; *P. setaceum* 'Burgundy Giant' Z 7–9

Cultivation: Grow in fertile, well-drained soil in full sun and use a dry mulch to insulate the roots in winter. Cut back top growth in early spring.

Phyllostachys
Bamboo

These elegant bamboos can serve as border or container specimens, as backdrops for smaller plants or as screening. Some are invasive, but their spread can be restricted by planting them in large containers sunk in the ground or by inserting deep barriers around their roots. New bamboo shoots can be cut off as they emerge. Handsome and generally well-behaved forms include *P. flexuosa*, the aptly named zigzag bamboo, *P. aurea* (fishpole or golden bamboo) and *P. aureosulcata f. auriocaulis*, both of which have golden yellow canes at maturity. The black bamboo, *P. nigra*, has greenish brown canes that turn an impressive lacquer-black with age – a truly dramatic plant.

Height and spread: 2–6m (6–20ft) x indefinite; less when grown in containers

Hardiness: Hardy/Z 6–10

Cultivation: Grow in fertile, well-drained but moisture-retentive soil in sun or light shade.

Pleioblastus
Bamboo

These slow-creeping bamboos make fine container plants where space is restricted. The white-striped low-growing *P. variegatus* looks well at the front of a border in an oriental setting and the taller, yellow-banded *P. auricomus* syn. *P. viridistriata* adds sparkle to dark and richly coloured perennials such as *Geranium psilostemon*. Both blend well with ferns and broad-leaved architectural plants in a cool leafy border.

Height and spread: *P. variegatus* 75cm x 1.2m (40in x 4ft); *P. auricomus* 90cm–1.5m x 1.2–1.5m (3–5 x 4–5ft)

Hardiness: Hardy/*P. auricomus* Z 8–10; *P. variegatus* Z 7–11

Cultivation: Grow in fertile, moisture-retentive soil, including clay, in sun or light shade. Cut back last year's stems in early spring to ground level to promote colourful new

Above: Stipa gigantea

foliage. Curb unwanted spread by cutting through roots with a spade and discarding the unwanted material.

Stipa spp.

The stipas range in character from stand-alone specimens such as *S. gigantea*, otherwise known as golden oats, to the diaphanous *S. tenuissima*, whose tussocks of light green fading to biscuit, hair-like foliage are a perfect foil for so many flowering and foliage perennials. Its common names include Mexican feather grass and the descriptive 'pony tails'. *S. gigantea* adds height to a flat area of paving or gravel but has the advantage over shrubs and conifers of being see-through. Dot randomly through an area of low-growing plants, or use singly as a striking accent in a courtyard. The blue-green leaves of *S. calamagrostis* are topped in summer by feathery, arching, silvery buff flower panicles.

Height and spread: *S. gigantea* 2.5 x 1.2m (8 x 4ft); *S. tenuissima* 60 x 30cm (2 x 1ft); *S. calamagrostis* 1 x 1.2m (3 x 4ft)

Hardiness: Hardy/Z 7–10

Cultivation: Needs well-drained soil and a sunny spot. Cut back *S. tenuissima* and *S. calamagrostis* in early spring and tidy the evergreen basal clumps of *S. gigantea* after removing spent flower stems. Remove unwanted seedlings of *S. tenuissima*.

Above: Pleioblastus auricomus

Above: Phyllostachys nigra

Above: Stipa tenuissima

EVERGREENS

Evergreen shrubs, ground cover plants and foliage perennials are invaluable for the smaller garden where every part is on show year round. They help to create a feeling of restfulness and permanence, adding to the structure of the space, especially in the form of clipped hedges and topiary. Plain-leaved subjects act as a foil for brighter, more flamboyant seasonal plants.

Above: Choisya ternata *'Sundance'* *creates a bright splash in a dull corner.*

Abelia
Glossy abelia

With its small, slightly glossy, dark green foliage, *Abelia* x *grandiflora* makes a handsome rounded shrub. It enjoys the shelter of a courtyard and rewards care with an abundance of dainty, tubular, fragrant, pink-tinged-white flowers between midsummer and autumn (fall). The somewhat less vigorous, semi-evergreen, arching form, 'Francis Mason', has attractive gold leaves streaked green.

Height and spread: 2.5 x 3m (8 x 10ft)
Hardiness: Borderline hardy/ Z 6–9
Cultivation: Fertile, well-drained soil in sun and shelter.

Bergenia
Elephant's ears

This plant tolerates less than ideal conditions from shade and heavy clay to heat and drought but generously rewards any extra care. The large, rounded and glossy evergreen leaves carpet the ground and contrast well with grassy leaves. In spring, stout flower heads packed with waxy tubular blooms in shades of white ('Bressingham White', 'Silberlicht'), through pink ('Wintermärchen') to deep magenta red ('Morgenröte', 'Abendglut') appear. Many develop striking red or deep mahogany leaf tints in winter.

Height and spread: 30–45 x 45–60cm (12–18 x 18–24in)

Hardiness: Hardy/Z 3–8
Cultivation: Tolerates a wide range of conditions but prefers fertile, moisture-retentive, humus-rich soil and sun. Remove dead leaves before flowering. Mulch with well-rotted manure or garden compost (soil mix) and periodically divide in early spring.

Buxus sempervirens
Common box, boxwood

Along with yew, this is one of the classic topiary plants, widely used for balls, domes, cones and spirals as well as for formal hedging. The dwarf form *Buxus sempervirens* 'Suffruticosa' makes intricate knots and parterres. Box works well in containers sited in shady, sheltered courtyards. Some cultivars of *Buxus microphylla*, e.g. 'Green Pillow', develop softly rounded forms without clipping. *Buxus sempervirens* 'Elegantissima' has creamy-white variegated leaves.

Height and spread: Dependent on shaping
Hardiness: Hardy/Z 6–8 (*B. microphylla* 7–9)

Cultivation: Clip in late spring/early summer. Remove all dead foliage and clippings to lessen risk of box blight. Grow in humus-rich, preferably slightly alkaline soil in light shade. Water containers well in summer. Feed with half strength liquid fertilizer to avoid scorching, or mulch with garden compost (soil mix).

Choisya ternata 'Sundance'
Mexican orange blossom

A buttery yellow leaved version of the Mexican orange blossom, 'Sundance' is not so floriferous. Flowers are open, white and fragrant. This shows its colour best in light shade, such as against a north-facing wall. Bright sunshine and frost can bleach or scorch the younger leaves, so shelter plants from cold snaps and intense midday heat.

Height and spread: 2 x 2m (6 x 6ft)
Hardiness: Hardy/Z 8–10
Cultivation: Shelter and light shade preferred. Improve dry soils prior to planting.

Above: Abelia *x* grandiflora

Above: Bergenia *cultivar*

Above: B. sempervirens *'Suffruticosa'*

Above: Euonymus fortunei

Above: Heuchera *cultivar*

Above: Laurus nobilis

Above: Photinia x fraseri

Escallonia laevis 'Gold Brian'
Hopley's gold

'Gold Brian' and its variegated counterpart 'Gold Ellen' are gems for the year-round garden. Both form compact domes of neat, golden yellow to lime green leaves, and in mid-summer have plentiful clusters of small, rich pink flowers.
Height and spread: 1.5 x 1.5m (5 x 5ft)
Hardiness: Borderline hardy/Z 7
Cultivation: Best in light shade, though the sun brings out golden tones. Any reasonably fertile soil. Prefers shelter.

Euonymus fortunei
Wintercreeper

Invaluable as 'fillers', for containers or as ground cover, variegated forms of *E. fortunei* such as the green and white 'Emerald Gaiety' and gold-splashed 'Emerald 'n' Gold' light up the garden in winter. The plain, glossy-leaved *E. japonicus* is upright and less hardy but adds a Mediterranean touch. Its white or gold variegated forms include 'Ovatus Aureus'.
Height and spread: 60cm (2ft) x indefinite; *E.* 'Ovatus Aureus' 3 x 1.5m (10 x 5ft)
Hardiness: *E. fortunei* hardy/ Z 5–9; *E. japonicus* half hardy/ Z 7–9
Cultivation: Any reasonably fertile soil. 'Emerald Gaiety' keeps variegation well in shade.

Heuchera
Coral bells

Now available in a wide range of subtly different forms, heucheras offer attractively coloured ground cover. These evergreen perennials have maple leaf foliage sometimes with ruffled or frilled edges and airy blooms from late spring. Deep purple-reds include 'Plum Pudding' and 'Chocolate Ruffles'. 'Pewter Moon' is overlaid with silvery marbling. There are also lime green and amber-coloured forms.
Height and spread: 40 x 30cm (16 x 12in)
Hardiness: Hardy/Z 4–8
Cultivation: Grow on fertile, moisture-retentive soil in sun or light shade. Remove fading heads of flowering heucheras and cut back damaged foliage in spring. Susceptible to vine weevil larvae.

Ilex aquifolium
Holly

The hollies are tolerant evergreens, usually with spiny leaves. Though they can eventually grow into trees, they can be clipped for hedging or simple topiary figures such as cones, domes and standards. Many selections have brightly coloured variegation. Only female forms will berry, and most need to be in the vicinity of a male. *Ilex* 'J.C. van Tol' and a few others are self-fertile.

Height and spread: To 3 x 3m (10 x 10ft), but depends on the form and/or pruning
Hardiness: Hardy/Z 6–9
Cultivation: Sun or shade. Use loam-based potting compost (soil mix) and large, heavy containers.

Laurus nobilis
Sweet bay

The bay can be grown either as a tree or shrub, its stiff, matt green crinkle-edged leaves having a sweet aroma. Clip to form a ball, cone or standard.
Height and spread: 3 x 3m (10 x 10ft), or less, depending on pruning
Hardiness: Borderline hardy/ Z 8–10
Cultivation: Use potting compost (loam-based soil mix) for containers and place in sun or light shade. Clip in early summer.

Ligustrum delavayanum
Delavayanum privet

Similar to clipped box, this small-leaved privet is used for figurative and geometric topiary forms. Turn potted topiary regularly to avoid it developing bald patches on the shaded side.
Height and spread: Depends on clipping
Hardiness: Borderline hardy/ Z 8–9
Cultivation: Clip in summer. Needs good drainage and best sheltered from cold, drying winds.

Photinia x *fraseri* 'Red Robin'
Fraser's photinia

This vigorous shrub produces flushes of glossy red leaves in spring or after pruning. It can make a large background shrub when left to its own devices or can be shaped into an attractive multi-stemmed form with domed head or lollipop standards. *Photinia serratifolia* 'Curly Fantasy' has wavy-edged leaves.
Height and spread: 4 x 4m (13 x 13ft) if not pruned
Hardiness: Borderline hardy/Z 7–9
Cultivation: Grows on most soils provided drainage is good. Spring growth may be frosted. Cut back to living wood.

Taxus baccata
Yew

One of the traditional evergreens used for topiary and green architecture, e.g. castellated hedging, archways and turrets. The surface of well-clipped yew resembles dressed stone in all but colour. Perfect for the formal or traditional garden, and shade tolerant. The Irish yew, *T .b.* 'Fastigiata', has a columnar profile; the slow- growing 'Standishii' makes a narrow, gold-variegated column.
Height and spread: Dependent on size and shape of topiary
Hardiness: Hardy/Z 6–9
Cultivation: Grow on well-drained soil in sun or shade. Improve dry soils before planting.

SCENTED AND AROMATIC PLANTS

Scent introduces another dimension. Try planting herbs such as rosemary and lavender close to paths where their fragrance will be released as you pass by. Different scents create different moods: the scents of roses and honeysuckle suggest a morning in the country, while the heady perfumes of lilies and tobacco plants can transform a sunny courtyard into a sultry paradise.

Above: Brugmansia, *also known as Angel's trumpets, has a heady evening perfume.*

Brugmansia x *candida*
Angels' trumpets, datura

All parts of this exotic plant are poisonous. Huge, trumpet-like flowers hang down from summer to autumn (fall), at night giving off an intoxicating fragrance. Some forms have white, yellow or apricot flowers.
Height and spread: 1.5 x 1.5m (5 x 5ft) or more
Hardiness: Tender/Z 10
Cultivation: Grow in fertile, well-drained soil in full sun. Trim potted specimens and keep frost-free in winter.

Choisya ternata
Mexican orange blossom

This evergreen shrub has aromatic leaves and scented white flowers in late spring. It gives a topiary effect without pruning. 'Aztec Pearl' has elegant narrow leaflets.
Height and spread: 2 x 2m (6 x 6ft)
Hardiness: Hardy/Z 8–10
Cultivation: Grow in fertile, well-drained soil. Choisyas tolerate moderate shade, but flower best in full sun.

Jasminum
Jasmine

The jasmines have a sweet, heady scent that epitomizes summer. In cold areas grow *J. officinale*, trained against a warm wall or over a pergola if winter temperatures drop only a little below freezing. The tender, pink-budded *J. polyanthum* flowers spring to summer in frost-free courtyards.
Height and spread: To 3 x 3m (10 x 10ft)
Hardiness: *J. officinale* borderline hardy/Z 7–10; *J. polyanthum* tender/Z 9–10
Cultivation: Grow in well-drained, fertile soil in sun or part shade.

Lathyrus odoratus
Sweet pea

This climbing annual varies in strength of fragrance. The highly scented old-fashioned varieties have made a comeback recently, though their colour range is limited. Train on obelisks or garden cane (stake) wigwams to give height. Pick or deadhead the flowers regularly to encourage more blooms.

Height and spread: To 2 x 2m (6 x 6ft)
Hardiness: Hardy/Z 1–11
Cultivation: Grow in any fertile, moisture-retentive soil in full sun. Sow in late autumn (fall) for early blooms or spring.

Lavandula
Lavender

Lavender flowers are adored by bees. English lavender, *L. angustifolia*, a cottage garden favourite, includes forms such as 'Hidcote' (deep purple); 'Nana Alba' (a compact white) and *L.* x *intermedia* (robust, with broader leaves and lavender flowers). Slightly less hardy is French lavender, *L. stoechas.*
L. pedunculata subsp. *pedunculata* (syn. *L. s.* 'Papillon') flowers for months on end.
Height and spread: 45 x 45cm (18 x 18in) or more

Hardiness: Hardy/Z 6–9; *L. stoechas* Z 7–9
Cultivation: Grow in very well-drained soil, especially lime-rich or poor gravelly ground, in full sun. Keep bushy by clipping off old flower stems in early spring or as flowers fade in summer.

Lilium
Lily

In pots, try the tall trumpet-flowered African Queen Group (soft apricot), Pink Perfection Group or *L. regale*, with richly scented, white, waxy blooms, flushed purple outside. The Madonna lily, *L. candidum*, has white, widely flared blooms. Two more whites of note are *L. formosanum* with strong purple flushes on the outside of the blooms and *L. longiflorum*, which scents the night air.
Height: To 60–120cm (2–4ft)

Above: Jasminum officinale

Above: Lathyrus odoratus

Above: Lonicera periclymenum

Above: Nicotiana *Domino Series*

Above: Pittosporum tobira

Above: Rosemarinus officinalis

Hardiness: Hardy/Z 4–9
Cultivation: Provide good drainage, a cool root run and sunshine. Plant *L. candidum* shallowly in alkaline soil; *L. formosanum* needs moist, acid soil; *L. regale* is tolerant. Plant bulbs deep, using loam-based compost (soil mix) for pots.

Lonicera periclymenum
Honeysuckle
Honeysuckles are renowned for their scent, but not all are fragrant. *L. periclymenum* is one of the best for fragrance from dusk, and has two main forms: 'Belgica', sometimes called Early Dutch honeysuckle, has pink and red flowers in early summer; 'Serotina' (Late Dutch) has purple and red flowers from midsummer to autumn (fall). Both bear glistening red berry clusters. Honeysuckles can cover a pergola, make a scented arbour, or grow through a tree.
Height and spread: To 4 x 4m (13 x 13ft)
Hardiness: Hardy/Z 5–9
Cultivation: Any soil that is not too dry, with roots in the shade.

Matthiola
Stock
Most stocks can be treated as annuals or biennials, depending on the time of sowing. The white, pink, lavender or crimson flowers are lovely in cottage garden schemes. Brompton stocks are biennials; selected

strains include double forms and dwarfs. The Ten Week Series flower ten weeks after sowing, so staggering can result in a long season. Scatter seed of the headily night-scented *M. longipetala* subsp. *bicornis* amongst other plants.
Height and spread: 30 x 20cm (12 x 8in)
Hardiness: Hardy/Z 6
Cultivation: Grow in any soil in full sun. Sow seed from summer onward for flowers the following year and from late winter for flowers the same year.

Nicotiana x *sanderae*
Tobacco plant
As day temperature drops, the flowers of the tobacco plant release an incense-like fragrance. Tall, old-fashioned seed mixtures produce pastel flowers with a heady scent. Modern single-colour selections and dwarfs are less fragrant.
Height and spread: 30–90 x 25cm (12–36 x 10in)
Hardiness: Half hardy/Z 7
Cultivation: Grow in any soil in sun or light shade. Sow in a propagator in early spring.

Pittosporum tobira
Japanese pittosporum
This species has handsome, glossy foliage and clusters of sweetly scented star-shaped white flowers in late spring to early summer, later turning yellow. It makes a hedge in a

frost-free garden; elsewhere try growing it in containers.
Height and spread: 2 x 1.5m (6 x 5ft)
Hardiness: Borderline hardy/ Z 8–10
Cultivation: Grow in good, loam-based compost (soil mix) in sun or light shade. Prune or shape in late spring.

Rosa
Rose
There is a wide variation in the scent of roses; some have none and others release a fresh, spicy or deep, musk-like perfume. The climber 'Louise Odier', flowering in midsummer has strongly scented, double, bright pink flowers. 'Zéphirine Drouhin', also climbing, with magenta flowers, has a warmer fragrance. The Bourbon shrub rose 'Alba Semiplena' has very fragrant, milky white flowers.
Height and spread: Climbers to 3 x 3m (10 x 10ft); bush types 1–2 x 1–2m (3–6 x 3–6ft)
Hardiness: Hardy/Z 4–9
Cultivation: Grow in fertile, well-drained soil, ideally in full sun. Prune in early spring, if necessary. Deadhead regularly.

Rosmarinus officinalis
Rosemary
The aroma of this Mediterranean sub-shrub and culinary herb is especially strong in hot, dry weather. The species and its forms, with grey-blue to gentian blue flowers, bloom from mid-spring into summer. They can become long and bare, but respond well to light pruning.
Height and spread: To 2 x 1m (6 x 3ft)
Hardiness: Hardy/Z 7–9
Cultivation: Grow in free-draining, light soil in full sun. Prune after flowering.

Trachelospermum jasminoides
Star jasmine
An evergreen climber with pinwheel-shaped, divinely scented, white flowers in summer. More or less hardy, some form of winter protection is advisable in cold areas.
Height and spread: To 9 x 9m (29 x 29ft)
Hardiness: Borderline hardy/ Z 8–10
Cultivation: In containers, grow in loam-based compost (soil mix) in sun or light shade with support.

TROPICAL PLANTS

If you want to add a touch of the exotic and conjure scenes of tropical holiday destinations, then add some of the sculptural and large-leaved plants that are described here. Many of them are surprisingly hardy grown within the sheltered confines of a courtyard. For others, you can often provide sufficient protection from cold by wrapping in situ or mulching.

Above: Agapanthus *'Loch Hope' is one of the more hardy and compact cultivars.*

Above: Astelia chathamica

Above: Cordyline australis

Above: Dicksonia antarctica

Above: Eucomis bicolor

Acacia dealbata
Silver wattle, mimosa
The acacias are pretty trees or large shrubs with ferny, grey-green leaves and masses of fluffy, duckling-yellow flowers in late winter. *A. dealbata* is a delightful choice for a sheltered courtyard. Acacias are fast growers, but take well to pruning and are good wall shrubs.
Height and spread: 6 x 4m (20 x 13ft); less in a container or if wall-trained
Hardiness: Half hardy/Z 8–10
Cultivation: Grow in lime-free soil in full sun.

Agapanthus
African lily
These beautiful plants produce lush clumps of large, strap-shaped leaves before the heads of trumpet-like flowers appear in late summer. Spectacular but tender, so requiring winter protection, is *A. africanus*, an evergreen with deep blue flowers on tall stems. The borderline hardy *A. campanulatus* and forms are

a safer bet, or go for the truly hardy hybrids such as the deep blue *A.* 'Loch Hope'.
Height and spread: 60–120 x 60cm (2–4 x 2ft)
Hardiness: Borderline hardy/ Z 7–10
Cultivation: Grow in fertile, reliably moist (but not boggy) soil in full sun. Protect with a dry winter mulch in cold areas.

Astelia chathamica
Silver spear
This New Zealand native looks like a metallic version of phormium. Though plants do sometimes flower in cultivation, it is the upright to arching strap-shaped leaves of silvery sage green that are the main feature of this striking evergreen perennial. *A nervosa* also has small, star-shaped flowers.
Height and spread: 1.2 x 1m (4 x 3ft)
Hardiness: Frost hardy/Z 8
Cultivation: Best in containers for ease of moving to shelter in winter. Use a moisture-retentive, peaty soil mix. Water freely in

summer but keep the plants very much drier in winter. This increases their hardiness. Grow in sun or light shade.

Canna x generalis
Canna lily
These exotic-looking plants have large upright leaves, often overlaid with bronze. The sumptuous, orchid-like flowers come in a range of colours, including bright red, white, yellow, orange and salmon, and appear from late summer to autumn (fall). Like dahlias, they can be lifted and overwintered in cold areas.
Height and spread: 1m x 50cm (3ft x 20in)
Hardiness: Half hardy/Z 7–10
Cultivation: Grow in fertile soil in full sun.

Chamaerops humilis
Dwarf fan palm
For warm courtyards only, this Mediterranean palm suckers from the base, making a bushy plant, well clothed with exotic-looking leaves of glossy green. It tolerates shade, and makes a

good choice for a courtyard. Sometimes grown as a houseplant or conservatory (porch) plant in cold climates, it is an impressive specimen.
Height and spread: 3 x 2m (10 x 6ft)
Hardiness: Half hardy/Z 9–10
Cultivation: Grow in fertile, well-drained soil in sun or light shade.

Cordyline australis
Cabbage palm
Often seen as a street tree in warm areas, the cabbage palm has a straight trunk topped with a symmetrical head of blade-like leaves, the central ones stiffly erect, the outer ones splaying outward and downward. Selections with reddish purple or variegated leaves are much less hardy.
Height and spread: 3 x 1m (10 x 3ft), sometimes more in both directions
Hardiness: Half hardy to frost hardy/Z 9
Cultivation: Grow in fertile, well-drained soil in sun. Remove dying leaves at the base of the crown. Excellent pot plant.

Dicksonia antarctica
Tree fern

These are the plants of the moment: dramatic as single specimens and when grown in groups. Tree ferns will thrive in large pots in a sheltered, ideally lightly shaded spot. In cold areas, pack the dormant crowns with straw or some other dry material in winter.

Height and spread: 2 x 4m (6 x 13ft)
Hardiness: Half hardy/Z 10
Cultivation: Grow in fertile soil or soil mix, preferably enriched with leaf mould.

Eucomis bicolor
Pineapple plant

This plant has pineapple-like flowers, with a tuft of green leaves at the top. Thriving in pots, it does best in a sheltered spot. It produces pale green or white flower spikes from late summer to early autumn (fall).

Height and spread: 20–30 x 60–75cm (8–12 x 24–30in)
Hardiness: Borderline hardy/ Z 8–10
Cultivation: Grow in moderately fertile, well-drained soil in full sun. Protect in winter.

Melianthus major
Honey bush

One of the most handsome of all foliage plants, this has divided, soft, silvery-grey leaves. It is best grown against a wall in cold areas. Although shrubby, it behaves more like a herbaceous perennial in cold districts, dying back to ground level. Ideal for giving height to plantings of cannas, dahlias and half hardy annuals.

Height and spread: 2.5 x 2m (8 x 6ft)
Hardiness: Half hardy/Z 9–10
Cultivation: Grow in any fertile, well-drained soil in sun. In cold regions apply a dry mulch such as straw or bracken to insulate the roots.

Musa basjoo
Japanese banana

Bananas are grown for their exotic-looking, paddle-shaped, fresh green leaves. Away from the tropics any fruit produced is unlikely to ripen. The arching leaves create a jungle atmosphere. Also consider *Ensete* cultivars (Abyssinian banana).

Height and spread: 1.5 x 1.5m (5 x 5ft), or more in favourable conditions
Hardiness: Borderline hardy/ Z 9–10
Cultivation: Grow in fertile soil in full sun. In cold areas pack trunk loosely with dry straw in autumn (fall) as frost protection.

Phormium
New Zealand flax

Phormiums are handsome perennials with blade-like leaves that arch elegantly over. They need winter protection in cold areas. One of the tougher selections, *P. tenax* Purpureum Group has bronze-purple leaves. A wide array of creamy yellow- and coppery pink-leaved forms is available – these require warmth and shelter.

Height and spread: 2 x 2m (6 x 6ft) or more; dwarf forms generally within 1 x 1m (3 x 3ft)
Hardiness: Borderline hardy/ Z 8–10
Cultivation: Grow in drained but moisture-retentive soil. Use a loam-based compost (soil mix) for containers. Sun or light shade. Protect with a deep dry mulch in cold areas.

Trachycarpus fortunei
Chusan palm

The hardiest palm, this is useful for bringing the exotic to cool-region courtyards. Stiff, pleated leaves making impressive fans can be 75cm (30in) across.

Height and spread: To 3 x 1.5m (10 x 5ft)
Hardiness: Borderline hardy/ Z 8–10

Cultivation: Grow in loam-based compost (soil mix) and place in sun or light shade. Shelter plants from strong winds in winter.

Washingtonia filifera
Desert fan palm

This tender palm is similar in appearance to *Trachycarpus fortunei* but with a more open habit – leaf stalks can be 1.5m (5ft) long or even more on mature specimens – and a trunk swollen at the base. As the lower leaves die back, a 'thatch' develops on the trunk. This is a fire risk and so should be removed. Suited to planting in dry urban landscapes.

Height and spread: 3 x 1.5m (10 x 5ft), or more in either direction
Hardiness: Tender/Z 9–10
Cultivation: Use loam-based compost (soil mix) with added leaf mould and sharp sand, and place plants in full sun.

Above: Phormium tenax *cultivar*

Above: Melianthus major

Above: Trachycarpus fortunei

HEAT-LOVING PLANTS

In areas that have hot dry summers or corners of the courtyard that are sizzling sun traps, you must have a set of plants that will thrive as the temperature climbs and will not create unreasonable demands for watering. The following selection includes brightly coloured sun-worshippers, intricately shaped and textured succulents and striking architectural plants.

Above: *The blue heads of* Cynara cardunculus *can be cut for drying.*

Above: Bougainvillea glabra

Agave americana
Century plant
These eventually huge succulents, with rosettes of leathery, waxy-coated, toothed-edged leaves, also have spectacular flower spikes. Flowering results in the death of the central rosette, but fresh plants develop around the base. Remove and grow on until they too reach flowering size. *A. a.* 'Marginata' has leaves edged with creamy yellow – a variegation reversed on 'Mediopicta'.
Height and spread: 2 x 2m (6 x 6ft)
Hardiness: Tender/Z 9–10
Cultivation: Use standard cactus potting compost (soil mix) and site in full sun. Provide winter protection in cold areas.

Bougainvillea
Paper flowers
These are rampant, thorny-stemmed climbers for warm climates only. The 'flowers' – actually coloured bracts – are long-lasting. *B.* x *buttiana* is a large group of hybrids with flowers in shades of white, yellow, purple or red. The species *B. glabra* has white or magenta flowers, which often have wavy edges.
Height and spread: 10 x 10m (33 x 33ft)
Hardiness: Half hardy/Z 9–10
Cultivation: Grow in fertile, well-drained soil in full sun or light shade. Train over pergolas or against walls. Can be planted in large pots to grow up posts where there is no soil border.

Cistus
Rock rose
These Mediterranean shrubs have sticky, aromatic shoots and a succession of crinkled, papery flowers in summer. *C.* x *aguilarii* 'Maculatus' has white flowers, blotched blackish maroon at the centre, and *C.* x *pulverulentus* has rich cerise flowers.
Height and spread: To 1.2 x 1.2m (4 x 4ft)
Hardiness: Borderline hardy/ Z 7–9
Cultivation: Grow in very well-drained soil, including poor gravelly areas in sun.

Convolvulus cneorum
Silverbush
This beautiful plant is related to bindweed. The silky silver leaves alone make it worth growing, so the clear white flowers are an added bonus in summer. It revels in hot, dry conditions and, like many silver-leaved plants, looks best in gravel.
Height and spread: 60 x 60cm (2 x 2ft)

Above: Ipomoea indica

Hardiness: Hardy/Z 8–10
Cultivation: Grow in very well-drained soil, preferably gritty, in full sun.

Cynara cardunculus
Cardoon
A dramatic perennial, for use either as a specimen or in imposing groups at the back of a large border, if you have enough space. It has huge, jagged-edged leaves of silvery grey and, in summer, large, thistle-like flowers at the tops of sturdy stems.
Height and spread: 2 x 1.2m (6 x 4ft)
Hardiness: Half hardy/Z 9–10
Cultivation: Grow in well-drained soil in full sun.

Euphorbia characias
subsp. *wulfenii*
Spurge
This shrubby euphorbia is distinguished by its domed heads of lime green flowers that last for a long period over late spring and early summer. 'Lambrook Gold' has particularly vivid flowers but

Above: Pelargonium

Above: Passiflora *'Amethyst'*

Above: Plumbago auriculata

Above: Sempervivum *'Raspberry Ripple'*

those of 'John Tomlinson' are even more yellowish. Unnamed seedlings may not be so distinguished. Cut individual stems to the base after flowering, leaving new shoots to replace old. Handle with care as the sap is an irritant.

Height and spread: 1.5 x 1.5m (5 x 5ft)

Hardiness: Borderline hardy/ Z 7–10

Cultivation: Grow in well-drained soil, preferably in full sun, though this euphorbia tolerates light shade.

Ipomoea nil
Morning glory

Best known for its sky blue trumpet-like flowers, which last only a day, this annual climber also comes in purples, reds and white. *I. indica*, the Blue Dawn flower, has funnel-shaped, purple-blue flowers.

Height and spread: To 3–4 x 3–4m (10–13 x 10–13ft)

Hardiness: Tender/Z 10

Cultivation: Grow in moderately fertile, well-drained soil in sun.

Passiflora caerulea
Blue passion flower

Most passion flowers are hothouse plants, but the species described is reliably hardy in a sheltered spot in cold areas. The distinctive summer flowers, which are white with a central boss of violet filaments, are striking,

and are sometimes followed by fleshy egg-shaped yellow fruits. The selected form *P. c.* 'Constance Elliot' is a real stunner, with fragrant, creamy white flowers.

Height and spread: To 3 x 3m (10 x 10ft)

Hardiness: Borderline hardy/ Z 8–10

Cultivation: Grow in any fertile, well-drained soil in full sun. Protect in winter in cold areas. Provide support for tendrils.

Pelargonium
Pot geranium

These popular plants flower all summer long, in all shades of pink, salmon, purple, red and white. Use them in borders, in hanging baskets, window boxes and any kind of container. There are too many hybrids to mention individually, but pelargonium groups include ivy-leaved types with thick, shield-like leaves on trailing stems, ideal for troughs and baskets; zonal pelargoniums, for many people the typical pelargonium, have leaves banded or zoned a darker colour.

Height and spread: Usually to 45 x 45cm (18 x 18in)

Hardiness: Tender/Z 10

Cultivation: Grow in any well-drained soil in full sun. For pot plants, use any standard compost (soil mix) with added grit or perlite.

Plumbago auriculata syn. P. capensis
Cape leadwort

This South African gem is grown for its appealing sky blue flowers, produced over a long period in summer on a mound of lax stems. The plant does not climb unaided, but needs to be tied to a support. In cold areas, move containers into a conservatory (porch) over winter.

Height and spread: 1.5 x 1.5m (5 x 5ft), more in a favourable site

Hardiness: Tender/Z 9

Cultivation: Grow in well-drained soil in sun or light shade.

Sempervivum
House leek

Though not as showy as the maroon-black *Aeonium* 'Zwartkop' or blue-leaved *Echeveria*, these rosette-forming succulents have the advantage of being remarkably hardy and extremely drought tolerant. Coming in a very wide variety of purple-, red-, green- or grey-leaved species and cultivars, sometimes overlaid with a cobweb of pale hairs, each 'parent' becomes surrounded

by a colony of smaller individuals, which survive after the parent dies. These new offsets encrust the soil surface or spill out over the edges of pots.

Height and spread: 8–10 x 30cm (3–4 x 12in)

Hardiness: Hardy/Z 3–8

Cultivation: Grow in clay pots or alpine pans (wide, shallow terracotta pots) filled with a sharply draining, reasonably fertile compost (soil mix), and stand in full sun. Cut off old flower stems.

Yucca filamentosa
Adam's needle

This bold foliage plant, with its firm, blade-like leaves, has spikes of white flowers, usually in late summer to autumn (fall), but not necessarily every year. Yuccas create a symmetrical effect in a container. 'Bright Edge' is gold variegated.

Height and spread: 1 x 1m (3 x 3ft) (height doubled when in flower)

Hardiness: Hardy/Z 5–10

Cultivation: Use loam-based compost (soil mix), and place in full sun or very light shade.

SHADE-LOVING PLANTS

While it can seem that all the interesting plants need sun, many beautiful specimens will tolerate light or dappled shade. The ground beneath shrubs and climbers can be colonized with a handsome array of shade-loving foliage perennials such as hostas and ferns. And in heavily shaded courtyards, clusters of large planted containers make luxuriant displays.

Above: Leucothoe *'Scarletta' syn 'Zeblid'* *has rich red and mahogany foliage.*

Aucuba japonica
Spotted laurel

This shade-loving, pollution-tolerant shrub has several fine gold-splashed cultivars, and female forms such as 'Crotonifolia' also produce crops of large red berries. Few shrubs brighten up a gloomy corner in a city courtyard so well.

Height and spread: 2–2.5 x 2–2.5m (6–8 x 6–8ft)

Hardiness: Hardy/Z 7–10

Cultivation: Any reasonably fertile and moisture-retentive but drained soil. Cut off frost-damaged shoots mid-spring.

Begonia
Begonia

Shady containers and baskets rely on the floriferous but tender begonias for colour through summer into autumn (fall). Tuberous-rooted pendulous begonias come in shades of white, pink, red, orange and yellow. The orange *B. sutherlandii* is a dainty choice. New on the scene, 'Dragon Wing Red' has deep glossy green architectural leaves and copious scarlet blooms.

Height and spread: 60 x 30cm (2 x 1ft); *B. sutherlandii* 45 x 45cm (18 x 18in)

Hardiness: Frost tender to half hardy/Z 8–10

Cultivation: Grow in moisture-retentive compost (soil mix) sheltered from wind. Protect from vine weevil. Dead head regularly.

Cyrtomium
Holly fern

Less dainty than some other ferns, cyrtomiums are especially useful for providing a strong contrast to the more flamboyant plants in the courtyard border. *C. fortunei* has upright fronds, while *C. falcatum*, known as the Japanese holly fern, makes a good houseplant, although it can also be grown outdoors in sheltered areas.

Height and spread: 60 x 60cm (2 x 2ft)

Hardiness: *C. fortunei* hardy/ Z 6–9; *C. falcatum* borderline hardy/Z 7–9

Cultivation: Grow in fertile, moist but well-drained soil in any degree of shade.

Dryopteris
Male or Buckler fern

The dryopteris are robust ferns, invaluable for providing clumps of trouble-free greenery among other plants. *D. filix-mas*, the male fern, is technically deciduous, but usually does not die back completely in autumn (fall). *D. erythrosora* is best in a moist, sheltered site. Its triangular fronds are glossy coppery pink when young. *D. affinis* 'Cristata', known as the king of ferns, has striking upright fronds.

Height and spread: 60 x 60cm (2 x 2ft)

Hardiness: *D. filix-mas* hardy/ Z 4–8; *D. erythrosora* hardy/Z 5–9

Cultivation: Grow in fertile, humus-rich soil in shade.

Fatsia japonica
Japanese aralia, false castor oil plant

Fatsias are hardy enough for outdoor use in most areas. Their large, hand-like leaves give a tropical, jungle look. White pompon flowers in autumn (fall) are followed by black fruits.

Height and spread: 3 x 3m (10 x 10ft)

Hardiness: Borderline hardy/ Z 8–10

Cultivation: Grow in any well-drained soil. Prune in spring to remove frost-damaged wood and pull off dead leaves.

Fuchsia
Fuchsia

A huge group of tender and reasonably hardy species and cultivars ranging in height and form from tall shrubs suitable for

Above: Begonia sutherlandii

Above: Fuchsia *'Tom Thumb'*

Above: Cyrtomium fortunei

hedging to small pendulous plants for baskets. Individual flowers can be breathtaking and vary from slender tubes and single blooms with elegantly protruding stamens to sumptuous two-tone confections with semi or fully double flowers. Among the smaller borderline hardy fuchsias are the arching 'Lena' with white and magenta double blooms, the bushy single red and purple flowered 'Tom Thumb' and taller, similarly coloured 'Mrs Popple'.

Height and spread: 'Tom Thumb' 30 x 30cm (12 x 12in); 'Lena' 30–60 x 75cm (12–24 x 30in); 'Mrs Popple' 1 x 1m (3 x 3ft)
Hardiness: Frost hardy to borderline hardy/Z 9–11; 'Mrs Popple' Z 8
Cultivation: Grow in moisture-retentive but drained soil or compost (soil mix) and keep pots well watered in summer. Deadhead and liquid feed with flowering formula fertilizer.

Hosta
Hosta, plantain lily
Gradually increasing in size each year, hostas make striking specimens. They are like caviar to slugs, but growing in pots stood on gravel provides some protection. Moderately slug-resistant large-leaved hostas include *H. sieboldiana* 'Frances Williams', an old variety, with puckered, thick, glaucous green leaves, margined with creamy

Above: H. sieboldiana elegans

beige, and *H. sieboldiana* var. *elegans* with thickly puckered, glaucous, bluish-green leaves and almost white flowers.
Height and spread: To 60 x 60cm (2 x 2ft) or more, depending on variety
Hardiness: Hardy/Z 4–9
Cultivation: Grow in fertile, humus-rich, reliably moist soil.

Impatiens hybrids
Busy Lizzies
Flowering profusely in shade, these will brighten dull corners. They are difficult to raise from seed, so buy them as bedding plants or as 'plugs' in early spring. Colours include white, pink, red, purple and orange.
Height and spread: To 30 x 30cm (12 x 12in)
Hardiness: Tender/Z 10
Cultivation: Grow in moisture-retentive but drained fertile soil. Avoid overhead watering.

Lamium
Deadnettle
A groundcover perennial with evergreen foliage, 'White Nancy' combines silvery white leaves with short spikes of hooded white flowers. Good container plant.
Height and spread: 15 x 15cm (6 x 6in); roots as it grows
Hardiness: Hardy/Z 3–8
Cultivation: Sun or shade. Improve thin, dry soils with copious organic matter. Cut back periodically to encourage fresh foliage and flowering.

Above: Pieris japonica

Above: Impatiens *hybrid*

Leucothoe
Fetter bush
These ericaceous shrubs include the cream and pink marbled *L. fontanesiana* 'Rainbow', with its arching branches clothed in elegant tapered leaves and sprays of white, lily-of-the-valley like blooms in late spring. Relatively new on the scene are compact shrubs with much smaller, mahogany red-tinted leaves such as *L.* 'Scarletta', 'Carinella' and the compact crinkled leaf form *L. axillaris* 'Curly Red'. All suit shady courtyard containers. Foliage colour intensifies through autumn (fall) and winter.
Height and spread: 1.5 x 1.5m (5 x 5ft)
Hardiness: Fully hardy/Z 5–8
Cultivation: Requires ericaceous compost (acid soil mix). Shade preferred, though sun tolerated.

Pieris
Lily-of-the-valley bush
Pieris are woodland shrubs and so do best in a lightly shaded position on the patio. Attractive as the bell-like spring flowers are, most are grown for their foliage, most striking as the new growth appears in spring.

P. japonica 'Flaming Silver' has bright red new growth, edged with a pink that rapidly fades to silvery white. 'Blush' has pink buds opening white but retaining a pinkish cast. 'Valley Valentine' has deep purple-red flowers opening from crimson buds.
Height and spread: 2 x 2m (6 x 6ft)
Hardiness: Borderline hardy/ Z 7–9
Cultivation: Use ericaceous compost (acid soil mix) for containers, ideally with added leaf mould.

Polystichum
Shield fern
These evergreen ferns make useful container specimens. *P. munitum* (sword fern) has shining green fronds. *P. aculeatum* (hard shield fern) looks elegant through winter and the highly divided fronds of *P. setiferum* Divisilobum Group (soft shield fern) are lacy in effect.
Height and spread: 1 x 1m (3 x 3ft)
Hardiness: Hardy/Z 4–9
Cultivation: Grow in humus-rich, preferably alkaline soil in shade.

EDIBLE PLANTS

It is remarkably easy to raise vegetables and herbs, even on the tiniest terrace. At the simplest level, fill some pots or hanging baskets with herbs, salad leaves or tomatoes. Blueberries and figs both grow well in containers, and many fruit trees, including apples and plums, come in dwarf forms. Try growing a potted grapevine over a pergola and squashes or runner beans up a trellis screen.

Above: *Cherry tomatoes in patio pots are too delicious not to sample!*

EASY VEGETABLES

Many vegetables are suitable for growing on patios and in courtyards, either in containers or raised beds, and some are extremely decorative. A number of reliable varieties that crop well and have good pest and disease resistance are listed here, but for a wider choice, consult seed catalogues regularly. New varieties, including increasing numbers designed for container growing, are introduced each year.

Allium cepa
Onions

These are usually grown from 'sets'. These are produced by sowing onion seeds very thickly, which then grow into small plants that produce small bulbs (the 'sets'). Plant in autumn (fall) and spring to ensure continuity of cropping. 'Giant Zittau' is a good variety for autumn planting and keeps very well. Reliable varieties include 'Red Baron' and 'White Prince'. Don't try to store onions with a thick neck as they will rot.

Beta vulgaris Cicla Group
Swiss chard

Sow this decorative vegetable in late spring for cropping from late summer. Swiss chard has large, glossy, crinkled leaves with white stalks. Those of ruby chard are brilliant red and the leaf beat mixture Bright Lights has red, yellow, orange and white stems. Pick young leaves to eat raw in salads and steam or stir-fry larger leaves picked from the outside of plants. Cover crowns with a dry mulch for winter protection.

Brassica oleracea
Cabbage, kale, borecole

'Marner Early Red', with its beetroot- (beet-) red leaves, eaten raw or cooked, is one of the first cabbages to crop. 'Vertus' and the purple-tinged 'January King' are frost tolerant Savoy cabbages. 'Castello' and the quick-maturing pointed cabbage 'Greyhound' are for summer cropping. Curly kale or borecole provides 'greens' from autumn (fall) through till spring. Sow spring for summer transplanting.

Capsicum annuum
Sweet or bell pepper; chilli pepper

These need a long growing season in a sheltered spot. 'Redskin' is compact and will grow in pots on the patio; 'Bendigo' grows in an unheated greenhouse and other excellent varieties include 'Hungarian Wax', with long, pointed, yellow fruits, and 'Cayenne', with very hot fruits that can be used fresh or dried. Also try 'Gold Spike' and 'Serrano Chilli' as well as the patio pot chillies, 'Apache' and 'Fatalii'.

Cucurbita pepo
Courgettes (zucchini)

Don't put plants outside until the last frosts have passed unless you can protect them with cloches. Courgettes are usually grown as bushes whilst the related squashes, such as acorn, are often grown over supports. Sow under glass from late spring to early summer, harvesting from midsummer onwards for courgettes, late summer and autumn (fall) for squashes. Varieties of courgette include 'Ambassador', 'Burpee Golden Zucchini', 'Early Gem' and 'Gold Rush'.

Daucus carota
Carrot

Can be sown in succession for cropping throughout the year. 'Flyaway' is an early maincrop variety that has been bred for resistance to carrot root fly. Try the short cylindrical and round varieties e.g. 'Amsterdam Forcing', 'Sytan' and 'Parmex' in pots.

Lycopersicon esculentum
Tomato

The ideal patio crop, tomatoes revel in warm sunshine and thrive in large containers or growing bags. For cherry tomatoes try 'Super Sweet 100', 'Gardener's Delight', the yellow 'Sungold' or (if using hanging baskets) 'Tumbler'.

Phaseolus coccineus
Runner (green) beans

Grown as annuals and tolerating some shade, runner beans need to be trained on a structure such as a twiggy tripod. They have attractive flowers. Good varieties include 'Sunset' and 'Czar'. French beans can outperform runner beans in difficult conditions.

Solanum tuberosum
Potatoes

These are divided into early and maincrop types. Tubers are traditionally sprouted or chitted in a light, cool, well-ventilated place prior to planting, but can be planted as sold with similar

Above: *Onions*

Above: *Chilli peppers*

Above: *Runner beans*

Above: *Pears*

Above: *Grapevine*

Above: *Chives*

results. Grow new potatoes (earlies) in large, deep tubs, gradually adding more soil as the shoots appear. Crop when the plants begin to flower. 'Charlotte' is nice in salads.

CONTAINER GROWN AND WALL-TRAINED FRUITS

A sunny wall is a gift to any fruit-lover. Espaliers, cordons or fans make the most economical use of space, and trees can be bought ready-trained. If a wall is shaded for much of the day, try the Morello cherry.

Ficus carica
Figs

Figs thrive in containers, making them ideal patio crops. In cold areas, only the fruits that emerge right at the start of the season will ripen. Remove any small figs that appear in mid-summer and towards the end of the growing season. Protect by bringing pots under cover in colder areas.

Malus domestica
Apples

These thrive well in cold areas as they need low temperatures in winter to ensure good flowering.

Prunus cultivars
Plums

Plums are hardy in a range of climates. Grow hardy varieties in an open site, less-hardy types against a warm, sunny wall to protect the spring blossom from frost. Dessert plums include 'Victoria', 'Belle de Louvain', with large purple fruits, and sweetly flavoured 'Greengage'. Cooking plums include 'Laxton's Cropper' and 'Pershore Yellow'.

Prunus persica
Peaches

Peaches make excellent wall crops, but in cold districts the blossom needs shelter from early frosts. The related nectarines (*P. persica* var. *nectarina*) and apricots (*P. domestica*) have similar needs. In frost-prone areas, a plum can be a safer bet. Peaches and nectarines fan-trained against a wall provide a decorative feature but both need a warm, sunny protected site to thrive.

Pyrus communis
Pears

Like apples, pears are good in cold areas, since they also thrive on low winter temperatures. Pears need a reliably warm summer and autumn (fall) for the fruit to ripen fully. Look for varieties grafted on to dwarfing rootstocks if space in the courtyard is at a premium.

Vaccinium corymbosum
Blueberry

Best cropped in its second year – take off the flowers in the first year of pot growing to allow plants to strengthen. Grow in ericaceous compost (acid soil mix) and water well throughout summer as the crop develops. A range of varieties will ensure heavier yields and longer cropping times. Net against birds.

Vitis vinifera
Grapevine

These make handsome plants, whether trained against a wall or over a pergola, and can be grown solely for ornament. For edible crops, thin fruit trusses as well as the grapes within each truss to produce larger fruits.

HERBS AND SALAD LEAVES

Most herbs and salads can be grown in containers, making them ideal patio crops. Make sure some are within arm's reach of the kitchen door: it's so rewarding to pick a selection of fresh herbs from outside to use in cooking.

Herbs don't usually have high nutrient requirements so are undemanding and can be fed and watered sparingly. Sage, rosemary, thyme, marjoram and French tarragon are especially drought tolerant. Chives (*Allium schoenoprasum*) are also suitable for growing in a container, and the small pink flowers are a bonus. Mint is invasive, so is best kept to its own container, rather than mixing. Ensure you have plenty of potted parsley, coriander (cilantro) and basil waiting in the wings as these annual herbs tend to get used up quickly. The tall, architectural and feathery-leaved fennel and its annual relative dill are best grown in the ground.

Leafy vegetables suitable for growing on the patio include all varieties of lettuce, particularly the continental or cut-and-come-again types, which regrow after cutting, such as 'Bionda Foglia'. 'Little Gem' is a quick-growing dwarf that soon produces hearts. Mixtures of lettuce, endive, beetroot (beet), baby spinach, chicory and parsley will provide a delicious mixed salad. Coriander and rocket (arugula) add zest and the latter is best sown in succession from spring to late summer, keeping the ground well watered in hot weather to prevent plants running to seed.

SPRING PLANTS

Don't ignore the potential of deciduous shrubs and perennials in favour of an evergreen-based design. Such optimism is felt as early bulbs break the dark days of winter and presage the arrival of spring. Choose early flowers such as *Crocus chrysanthus*, *cyclamineus* daffodils and 'Tête à Tête', and follow with hardy dwarf tulip cultivars and *Muscari*. Elegant and flamboyant late tulips herald summer.

Above: *The vigorous Dutch crocus looks good planted in naturalistic drifts.*

Anemone
Windflower

The showy flowers of *A. coronaria* appear from late spring to early summer, depending on when they are started off. Plant a few pots together for a spectacular display. The two main hybrid groups are the double-flowered St Bridgid and single-flowered De Caen Group in red, pink, violet-blue or white. The dainty daisy-flowered *A. blanda* bloom from early to mid-spring, and though tubers are often sold as mixtures, planting single colours like 'White Splendour' creates more impact.
Height and spread: 30–40 x 15cm (12–15 x 6in)
Hardiness: Hardy/*A. coronaria* Z 8–10; *A. blanda* Z 6–9
Cultivation: Use loam-based potting compost (soil mix) and keep in a sunny spot.

Camellia
Camellia

Spring-flowering camellias are generally forms of *C. japonica* or the hybrid group *C. x williamsii*.

Above: Anemone coronaria

These shade-loving woodlanders produce showy blooms in white, pink and red, with a huge variety of flower forms, including single, double, peony and anemone forms.
Height and spread: To 3 x 3m (10 x 10ft), depending on the variety
Hardiness: Hardy/Z 7–9
Cultivation: Grow in lime-free, moisture-retentive but drained soil rich in organic matter. Tolerates sun, with some shelter from midday heat. Avoid a site receiving morning sun. Shelter from wind.

Crocus
Crocus

With their goblet-like flowers, crocuses are reliable spring heralds. Most sturdy garden varieties are grouped under the late winter-flowering *C. chrysanthus*, which includes 'Cream Beauty', 'Snow Bunting', the striped 'Ladykiller' and 'Advance' with yellow and violet blooms, or *C. vernus* with 'Jeanne d'Arc', a pure white, and the stripy purple 'Pickwick'

Above: Muscari armeniacum

Above: Leucojum vernum

being popular choices. Plant in drifts or in shallow bowls and troughs.
Height and spread: 8 x 5cm (3 x 2in)
Hardiness: Hardy/Z 3–8
Cultivation: Grow in any but waterlogged soil in sun.

Leucojum vernum
Snowflake

Looking like Tiffany lamps, the snowflakes are among the most elegant of the spring bulbs, with nodding, bell-like flowers on tall, narrow stems. Each petal is delicately marked with green or yellow. They are especially effective when planted overhanging water.
Height and spread: 35 x 15cm (14 x 6in)
Hardiness: Hardy/Z 4–8
Cultivation: Snowflakes like reliably moist soil in sun or light shade.

Magnolia stellata
Star magnolia

The shrubbiest of the magnolias, its slow rate of growth makes it ideal for even the smallest courtyard. The spidery white flowers open well before the leaves in early to mid-spring, but the shrub, with its airy habit, fades into the background when not in bloom.
Height and spread: 1.2 x 1.5m (4 x 5ft)
Hardiness: Hardy/Z 5–9
Cultivation: Grow in fertile, well-drained soil in sun; in frost-prone areas, some shelter from strong early morning sun at flowering time is desirable.

Muscari
Grape hyacinth

These charming bulbs are easy to grow and some spread like wildfire. *M. armeniacum* is the

Above: *Dwarf* Narcissus cyclamineus

Above: Rhododendron yakushimanum

most commonly grown species, with dense clusters of deep purple-blue flowers. The less vigorous *M. botryoides* 'Album' has slender spikes of scented white blooms.

Height and spread: To 20cm (8in) x indefinite

Hardiness: Hardy/Z 2–9

Cultivation: Grow in any well-drained soil in sun or light shade.

Narcissus
Daffodil

The huge range of hybrid forms are divided into groups according to their flower shape. The double-headed, white 'Thalia', lovely with fritillaries, and 'Tête-à-Tête', a reliable dwarf with very early, bright yellow, multi-headed blooms, are two of the best. The fragrant 'Actea' has white petals and short orange-rimmed cups. For fragrance also try the double cream 'Sir Winston Churchill'. The early, low-growing *cyclamineus* daffodils have swept back petals and a long narrow cup and include the weatherproof hybrids 'February Gold', 'Peeping Tom' and 'Jetfire'.

Height: *N. cyclamineus* 20cm (8in); *N.* 'Thalia' 30cm (12in); *N.* 'Tête-à-Tête' 15cm (6in); *N.* 'Actaea' 45cm (18in)

Hardiness: Hardy/Z 3–9

Cultivation: Grow in any well-drained soil, preferably in full sun.

Pulmonaria
Lungwort

Stems bearing clusters of gentian blue, pink, mauve or white bell-shaped blooms appear before the ground-covering leaves of this woodlander open fully. Some, like *P. saccharata* 'Mrs Moon', have a two-tone effect with pink buds opening to purple petals. The similarly coloured Argentea Group develop leaves that are almost completely silver. For white flowers and silver-spotted leaves try *P. officinalis* 'Sissinghurst'.

Height and spread: 30 x 60cm (12 x 24in)

Hardiness: Hardy/Z 4–8

Cultivation: Grow on moisture-retentive soil rich in organic matter in shade. In midsummer, cut foliage to ground level, feed and water to encourage a fresh flush of leaves to last through untill autumn (fall).

Rhododendron
Rhododendron

Though many of the species and hybrids would overwhelm a courtyard garden, dwarf evergreen rhododendrons, including the Japanese azaleas, are ideal. Most form neat, shallow domes with small glossy leaves often taking on red and purple tones and studded with bright

Above: Tulipa *'Queen of Night'*

blooms in mid- and late spring, e.g. *R.* 'Vuyk's Scarlet'. *Rhododendron yakushimanum* is a slow-growing, larger-leaved species, with a rounded habit, and the new growth is covered in an attractive cinnamon felting. The large blooms are white-tinged pink. Related are a series of compact and colourful hybrids known as Yaks.

Height and spread: *R.* 'Vuyk's Scarlet' 75cm x 1.2m (2½ x 4ft); *R. yakushimanum* 1.2–1.5 x 1.2–1.5m (4–5 x 4–5ft)

Hardiness: Hardy/Z 5–8

Cultivation: Grow in containers in ericaceous compost (acid soil mix) or in borders of humus-rich, lime-free soil in sun or light shade, avoiding hot, dry locations. Water pots well in summer, preferably using rainwater.

Tulipa
Tulip

Available in a vast array of sumptuous colours and forms, tulips are ideal for containers. 'Spring Green' is creamy white, broadly striped with green – a marked contrast to the almost black 'Queen of Night'. The dwarf *greigii* tulips are all easy to grow and include 'Red Riding Hood', with early scarlet blooms over maroon-striped leaves. Try with primroses, dwarf daffodils and blue violas. Particularly elegant are the later-flowering tall, lily-flowered tulips, including the golden yellow 'West Point'.

Height: To 60cm (2ft)

Hardiness: Hardy/Z 3–8

Cultivation: Grow in any drained soil in full sun with shelter from strong winds. Best results are often achieved by planting new bulbs each autumn (fall).

SUMMER PLANTS

As we spend more time outside, the colours, varied flower forms and perfumes of summer blooms heighten the sensual experience. The exuberance of early summer 'cottage garden' plants and the arrival of bees and butterflies sweeps away memories of winter. From mid-summer, tender perennials or patio plants add flamboyant touches to pots and planters and many perform well into the autumn.

Above: Salvia verticillata, *particularly 'Purple Rain', flowers through the summer.*

Allium
Ornamental onion

These produce striking heads of blue or purple, white or yellow flowers, followed by decorative seed-heads. The early summer-flowering *A. christophii* has large, lilac-purple flowers in spherical heads that glint with a metallic sheen. *A. hollandicum* 'Purple Sensation' has smaller, deep purple drumsticks.

Height and spread:
A. christophii 60 x 18cm (2ft x 7in); *A. hollandicum* 'Purple Sensation' 1m x 10cm (3ft x 4in)
Hardiness: Hardy/Z 6; *A. christophii* borderline hardy/Z 4–10
Cultivation: Grow in any well-drained soil in sun, though they will tolerate some shade.

Argyranthemum
Marguerite daisy

As well as the familiar marguerite daisy – a tender perennial with a profusion of single white daisy-like blooms and divided grey-green leaves – there are a host of others, some with double or anemone-centred blooms and coming in shades of yellow, pink and crimson. Compact plants are available for containers.
Height and spread: 30–100 x 30–100cm (1–3 x 1–3ft), depending on variety
Hardiness: Half hardy/Z 10–11
Cultivation: Grow in free-draining potting mix (soil mix) or fairly fertile border soil in full sun. Clip over to deadhead after each flush to maintain a bushy habit.

Brachyscome
Swan river daisy

The compact, mossy leaved *B. multifida* has powder-blue daisies and is a tender perennial, ideal for baskets. Recent breeding has created a range of pastel-coloured annual daisies with good drought resistance that work well in courtyard beds, e.g. the black-eyed Bravo Series (blue, purple and white blooms).
Height and spread: To 45 x 45cm (18 x 18in)
Hardiness: Half hardy/Z 8b–11
Cultivation: Grow in free-draining but moisture-retentive compost (soil mix) or drained, fertile soil in sun.

Cosmos atrosanguineus
Chocolate cosmos

Smelling of delicious melted chocolate, the single, blood-crimson flowers of velvety texture are produced over a long period from midsummer to autumn (fall). Site so that you can put your nose to the flowers!
Height and spread: 75 x 45cm (30 x 18in)
Hardiness: Borderline hardy/ Z 7–9
Cultivation: Grow in moderately fertile, well-drained soil in sun. Winter protection is advisable in cold districts. Excellent for pots.

Cosmos bipinnatus
Garden cosmos

With one of the longest flowering seasons of any annual, cosmos are of unquestioned value. Apart from the distinction of the glistening flowers and feathery foliage, they are excellent for cutting and make a fine show *en masse*.
Height and spread: To 1m x 45cm (3ft x 18in)
Hardiness: Half hardy/Z 9

Cultivation: Grow in any soil in sun. Seed can be sown *in situ* after frost has passed. Deadhead regularly to prolong the display.

Crocosmia
'Lucifer'
Montbretia

The king of crocosmias, this robust plant has stiff, pleated leaves with large heads of brilliant flame-red flowers from midsummer. The leaves are also effective in flower arrangements.
Height and spread: 1.2m x 8cm (4ft x 3in)
Hardiness: Borderline hardy/Z 5–9
Cultivation: Grow in any garden soils, in sun or light shade, but avoid sites that are too hot and dry or windy. Light staking may be necessary.

Dahlia cultivars

These plants bring colour and flamboyance to the late summer and early autumn (fall) garden. The current vogue is for dark-, bronze- or black-leaved cultivars. Flowers can be huge, cactus- or waterlily-like; pompons or balls, in eye-catching shades of white, cream, pink, yellow, orange, red and purple.
Height and spread: To 1.2m x 60cm (4 x 2ft), depending on the variety; dwarfs to 45cm/ 18in tall
Hardiness: Half hardy/Z 9
Cultivation: Grow in well-drained but rich, moisture-retentive soil, in full sun. Excellent in containers. Stake taller varieties. Pinch out the growing tips for bushiness and deadhead. Tubers may be left in the border in mild regions.

Above: Allium christophii

Above: Cosmos atrosanguineus

Above: Dahlia

Above: Tropaeolum majus

Above: Diascia 'Rupert Lambert'

Above: Lilium 'Eros'

Diascia
Twinspur

Recent breeding of both diascia and the related nemesia genus has created a range of colourful, long-flowering plants, many of which will survive the winter in a sheltered spot outdoors. Ideal for containers, diascias carry sprays of delicate shell-shaped blooms in shades of pink, orange and salmon. Brick pink *D.* 'Ruby Field' is one of the hardiest.

Height and spread: 25–30 x 60cm (10–12 x 24in)
Hardiness: Frost hardy/Z 7–9
Cultivation: Grow in moisture-retentive compost (soil mix) and deadhead any spent flower stems regularly. Given sharp drainage, survives winter as a basal carpet of evergreen leaves.

Hemorocallis 'Stella de Oro'
Daylily

A compact free-flowering daylily with grassy leaves and rounded flared blooms of golden yellow produced in early summer and repeating in flushes. Always neat and requiring little maintenance.

Height and spread: 30 x 45cm (12 x 18in)
Hardiness: Hardy/Z 4–9
Cultivation: Easily grown on moisture-retentive, fertile loam or clay in sun or light shade.

Knautia macedonica
Knautia

A stalwart perennial, flowering through the second half of summer, this knautia has deep crimson pincushion flowers on wiry stems that mingle perfectly with other blooms. For a range of colours grow 'Summer Pastels'.

Height and spread: 60–80 x 45–60cm (24–32 x 18–24in)
Hardiness: Hardy/Z 5–9
Cultivation: Any well-drained soil in full sun. Deadhead.

Lilium
Lily

Hybrid lilies such as the compact orange 'Enchantment' are the easiest to grow. More exotic examples include the scented turkscap types 'Black Beauty' (deep red) and 'Eros' (pinkish-orange). 'Brushmarks', an Asiatic hybrid, makes sturdy plants with large flowers – rich orange marked with red.

Height: To 1.2m (4ft)
Hardiness: Hardy/Z 4–8
Cultivation: Grow in well-drained soil in sun (ideally in a position where their roots are shaded). Suitable for containers.

Rhodanthemum hosmariense
No common name

This low, creeping, sub-shrubby plant with finely cut silvery green foliage seldom stops flowering. Wiry stems carry large white daisies with a bold yellow centre. 'African Eyes' is a petite, bushy form.

Height and spread: 15–30 x 30–45cm (6–12 x 12–18in)
Hardiness: Frost hardy/ Z 6–9
Cultivation: Grow in any free-draining soil in sun. Deadhead regularly.

Salvia
Ornamental sage

Salvias are a huge genus with many excellent plants. Drought resistant kinds include *Salvia* x *sylvestris* 'Mainacht', with slender branched spikes of dark purple-blue flowers, in early to midsummer. The later flowering *S. verticillata* 'Purple Rain' is looser in habit with abundant whorled blooms into autumn (fall).

Height and spread: 70 x 45cm (28 x 18in)
Hardiness: Hardy/Z 5–9
Cultivation: Grow in moderately fertile, well-drained soil in sun or light shade.

Tropaeolum majus
Nasturtium

These familiar annuals are among the easiest to grow. Vigorous trailing varieties are used in hanging baskets or trained as climbers, but modern compact forms and the dark-leaved, red-flowered 'Empress of India' are lovely in pots or alternatively for filling in around other plants.

Height and spread: To 3 x 3m (10 x 10ft) (trailing forms); other strains often within 30 x 30cm (12 x 12in)
Hardiness: Half hardy/Z 8
Cultivation: Grow in any well-drained, preferably poor, soil in full sun.

Verbena bonariensis
Purpletop vervain

Tall, rigid, lightly branched stems carry rounded heads of tiny violet-purple blooms. Self-seeding scatters plants through borders, but the effect is light and airy. The plant is a magnet for bees and butterflies, with flowers continuing through summer and well into autumn (fall).

Height and spread: 1.2–2m x 45cm (4–6 x 1½ft)
Hardiness: Frost hardy/Z 7–9
Cultivation: Any free-draining soil in full sun. Though the mother plant may die in winter, seedlings produce fresh crops.

AUTUMN PLANTS

With the shortening days and evenings, and mornings becoming cooler, summer draws to an end. Autumn compensates, with its rich foliage colours highlighting the remaining blooms and providing a backdrop for glistening fruits and berries. Many tender, summer-flowering plants continue till the frosts and some flowers emerge only late in the year, one final fling before the new cycle begins.

Above: *Some forms of Japanese maple (Acer palmatum) produce glowing autumn hues.*

Above: Cotoneaster horizontalis

Above: Aster x frikartii *'Mönch'*

Above: Cyclamen hederifolium

Acer palmatum
Japanese maple
The fleeting but vivid autumn (fall) leaf display varies depending on the weather. Soil type can make a difference, with most acers colouring best in acidic conditions. Plants in the A. p. var. *dissectum* group have dainty filigree foliage. A. p. 'Sango-kaku' has lacquer-red stems and golden yellow autumn foliage and is an excellent small multi-stemmed tree.
Height and spread: 1.2–8m (4–25ft), variety dependent
Hardiness: Hardy/Z 5–8
Cultivation: Grow in any soil, preferably leafy and fertile, with some overhead shade. Protect from winds and spring frosts.

Anemone x hybrida
Japanese anemone
These upright perennials bring elegance and a spring-like freshness to the late summer garden, with their white or pink dish-shaped flowers atop wiry stems and contrasting yellow stamens. Spreading to form large clumps in time, they are ravishing in the dappled light beneath deciduous trees. Cultivars include 'Lady Gilmour' and 'Honorine Jobert'.
Height and spread: 1.5m x 60cm (5 x 2ft)
Hardiness: Hardy/Z 6–8
Cultivation: Grow in moisture-retentive soil in shade or sun; lighter, drier soils are tolerated.

Aster x frikartii 'Mönch'
Aster
The flowers of this daisy-like perennial appear in late summer and early autumn (fall) and are violet blue with yellowish orange centres. 'Mönch' has long-lasting, lavender blue flowers from midsummer, is disease-resistant and doesn't require staking.
Height and spread: 70 x 40cm (28 x 16in)
Hardiness: Hardy/Z 5–9
Cultivation: Grow in well-drained yet moisture-retentive, moderately fertile soil in full sun.

Ceratostigma willmottianum
Hardy plumbago
This cobalt blue-flowered deciduous shrub with a low domed habit works wonderfully against the backdrop of autumn (fall) leaves. Blooming from late summer, its leaves start to turn red as autumn approaches.
Height and spread: 1 x 1.5m (3 x 5ft)
Hardiness: Hardy/Z 7–9

Cultivation: Grow in a sunny, well-drained spot. The plant is usually cut back by frost, so remove dead stems in spring close to ground level.

Cotoneaster
Cotoneaster
The cotoneasters are tolerant of many situations that other plants abhor. Among the best for late interest is deciduous herringbone cotoneaster, C. horizontalis. The leaves turn a vivid red before falling at the same time as the berries ripen to red. Another good choice for late colour is the evergreen, ground-covering C. salicifolius 'Gnom' with vivid red berries.
Height and spread:
C. horizontalis 1 x 1.5m (3 x 5ft), taller trained against a wall; C. s. 'Gnom' 30cm x 2m (1 x 6ft)
Hardiness: Hardy/Z 5–8
Cultivation: These shrubs with their varied size and habit are tolerant of a wide range of conditions, including cold and exposure. Remove unwanted seedlings.

Cyclamen hederifolium
Cyclamen

This little Mediterranean cyclamen, formerly *C. neapolitanum*, blooms mid- and late autumn (fall) in shades of pink or white. The first flowers appear as the heart-shaped, marbled leaves open out. These last for months, making attractive ground cover. Freely seeding, large colonies soon establish beneath trees and larger deciduous shrubs.
Height and spread: 10 x 15cm (4 x 6in)
Hardiness: Hardy/Z 5–9
Cultivation: Tolerant of a wide range of conditions but soil must be well drained. Needs summer shade. Mulch with leaf mould or ground composted bark when the leaves die down in summer.

Hibiscus syriacus
Hibiscus

These upright deciduous shrubs with their trumpet-shaped blooms, each with a boss of stamens protruding from the dark-hearted centres seem too exotic to be hardy. Colours range from dusky pink 'Woodbridge' and rich blue 'Bluebird' to white or purple, and plants flower from late summer into autumn (fall).
Height and spread: 2.5 x 1.5m (8 x 5ft)
Hardiness: Hardy/Z 6–9
Cultivation: Well-drained, neutral to mildly alkaline soil with maximum sun and shelter.

Hydrangea
Hydrangea

Though many of the shade-loving mop-head or lace-cap flowered *H. macrophylla* and *H. serrata* cultivars begin flowering in summer, the blooms mature, change colour and often reach a peak of beauty through autumn (fall). The summer-flowering *H. paniculata* types such as 'Pink Diamond' and 'Unique', with creamy white, lacy, cone-shaped heads, also frequently develop pink or red shading.
Height and spread: To 1–1.5 x 1–1.5m (3–5 x 3–5ft), depending on cultivar
Hardiness: Hardy/Z 6–8
Cultivation: Excellent in large pots. Use loam-based compost (soil mix) or plant in humus-rich, moisture-retentive soil. Flowers may be pink-purple or blue, depending on the soil – acid or ericaceous is necessary for blue tones. Leave papery flower heads on over winter and cut back very lightly in spring to a pair of swollen buds. *H. paniculata* may be pruned hard in spring.

Kniphofia
Red hot poker, torch lily

Together with the familiar burning poker effect of yellow deepening to orange or red, there are cultivars blooming into early autumn (fall) that have predominantly single-coloured blooms, like the greenish-yellow 'Percy's Pride' or flame 'Prince Igor'. The blooms of *K. rooperi* are egg-shaped and two-toned. Site the clump where early frosts won't mar the display.
Height and spread: Around 1–1.2m x 60cm (3–4 x 2ft), depending on the variety
Hardiness: Hardy/Z 5–6 (most pokers, although some are borderline)

Cultivation: Grow in soil that does not dry out in summer but that remains well drained in winter. Full sun.

Pyracantha
Firethorn

Among the toughest of garden plants, the firethorns are ideal for screening. They froth over with creamy white flowers in early summer, and develop clusters of orange, yellow or red berries in autumn (fall). Magnificent trained against a wall, but beware of planting them too near a walkway, as the stems are armed with barbarous spines. 'Orange Glow' has vibrant orange berries, while those of 'Soleil d'Or' are golden yellow.
Height and spread: 1.8 x 1.5m (6 x 5ft), more if wall-trained
Hardiness: Hardy/Z 6–9
Cultivation: Grow in almost any soil, in sun or moderate shade.

Rudbeckia fulgida
Orange coneflower

This plant makes a vivid display in autumn (fall), with stiff yellow-orange daisy flowers, each with a black eye, above mounds of dark green foliage. Leave the heads in place through winter in larger courtyard borders.
Height and spread: 60 x 30cm (2 x 1ft)
Hardiness: Hardy/Z 4–9
Cultivation: Grow in most soils in sun but avoid dry spots as the plant needs moisture.

Sedum spectabile
Ice plant

Above their fleshy, grey-green leaves, ice plants produce flat heads of pink flowers in autumn (fall), loved by butterflies and bees. The flowers last for a long period, gradually turning a rich brown. 'Herbstfreude' has darker brick pink blooms.
Height and spread: 45 x 45cm (18 x 18in)
Hardiness: Hardy/Z 4–9
Cultivation: Grow in reasonably drained soils, including clays in sun or light shade.

Sorbus
Rowan

The rowans are good trees for the urban courtyard, casting little shade and tolerant of pollution. *S. aucuparia* 'Fastigiata' is narrowly upright, useful where space is at a premium, with orange berries enhanced by red or yellow autumn (fall) leaves. 'Joseph Rock' is similar with amber berries. The Kashmir rowan, *S. cashmiriana*, has large, pearl-like white berries that persist after leaf fall. For a small space try the dainty *S. villmorinii* with ferny leaves and clusters of small pale pink berries turning crimson.
Height and spread: To 10 x 7m (33 x 23ft); *S. cashmiriana* 4 x 3m (13 x 10ft)
Hardiness: Hardy/Z 5–8
Cultivation: Grow in any well-drained soil in sun or light shade.

Above: Hibiscus syriacus *'Diana'*

Above: Kniphofia *'Alcazar'*

Above: Rudbeckia fulgida

WINTER PLANTS

While in winter the garden lacks the exuberance of warmer months, the skeletal structure of deciduous shrubs and trees makes a pleasing contrast with evergreen forms. The glowing reds of foliage and stems punctuate the greenery and highlight the predominantly yellow and white winter blooms. Sculptural seed-heads decorate the borders, and pots of early bulbs signal the start of the new gardening year.

Above: Skimmia japonica *'Rubella'* is a form with tight crimson cones of flower buds.

Above: Cyclamen coum

Betula utilis jacquemontii
Himalayan birch

A multi-stemmed specimen of this beautiful tree can become a striking focal point for the garden in winter when the bark peels to reveal the white trunks. Selected forms, e.g. 'Jermyns', are even more beautiful. Relatively slow growing.
Height and spread: 15 x 7.5m (49 x 24ft)
Hardiness: Hardy/Z 4–7
Cultivation: Grow on well-drained but moist soil in sun. Wash algae from the bark with a sponge and mild soapy water.

Clematis cirrhosa
'Freckles'
Fern-leafed clematis

One of very few winter-flowering climbers, this clematis has nodding, bell-like, creamy white flowers, spotted with maroon,

during any mild spell in winter, but is at its best as the season draws to a close. In sudden cold snaps, the foliage may acquire bronze tints.
Height and spread: 6 x 6m (20 x 20ft)
Hardiness: Hardy/Z 7–9
Cultivation: Grow in fertile, well-drained, ideally alkaline soil in sun or light shade. Best against a sunny wall in cold areas.

Cyclamen coum
Sowbread

The hardy cyclamen provides close ground cover in dry shade. The dainty flowers, with their back-swept petals, appearing in winter and early spring can be purple-violet, pink or, in the case of 'Album', white. The leaves are marbled.
Height and spread: 8 x 10cm (3 x 4in)

Hardiness: Hardy/Z 5–9
Cultivation: Grow in moderately fertile, moist but well-drained soil in partial shade; drier soils are tolerated.

Daphne bholua
Lokta

For fragrance in the sheltered winter garden, these reliable Himalayan daphnes are hard to beat. The upright stems are scattered with rounded clusters of waxy tubular flowers (white flushed pink and purple) in late winter. *D. b.* var *glacialis* 'Gurkha' is deciduous and slightly tougher than the evergreen 'Jacqueline Postill'.
Height and spread: 2 x 1.5m (6 x 5ft)
Hardiness: Borderline hardy/Z 7
Cultivation: Grow in sun or light shade on humus-rich, moisture-retentive ground or in large pots.

Erica carnea
Winter heath

Varieties of the lime-tolerant *E. carnea* and *E. x darleyensis* are invaluable as groundcover beneath deciduous shrubs in

Above: Daphne bholua

winter and make good pot specimens, acting as a foil for early bulbs. A range of pink and purple shades is available, but whites tend to be most popular. The carpeting *E. c.* 'Springwood White' blooms for weeks over fresh green foliage, while *E. x d.* 'Silberschmelze' is taller with cream-tipped growth in spring.
Height and spread: 'Springwood White' 20 x 55cm (8 x 22in); 'Silberschmelze' 30 x 75cm (12 x 30in)
Hardiness: Hardy/*Erica carnea* Z 6–8; *E. x darleyensis* Z 7–8
Cultivation: Grow in sun on humus-rich, moisture-retentive but drained soil.

Galanthus
Snowdrop

Among the first bulbs to flower in winter, snowdrops are universally loved. *G. nivalis* is the most usual species, but they hybridize so freely that there are many forms. 'Flore Pleno' has honey-scented double flowers, the tips touched with green. *G.* 'Atkinsii' has elongated petals and broad, grey-green leaves.

Above: E. carnea *'Eileen Porter'*

Above: Galanthus nivalis

Above: Helleborus orientalis

Height and spread: 10 x 10cm (4 x 4in)
Hardiness: Hardy/Z 3–9
Cultivation: Grow in reliably moist soil, preferably where they will be shaded when dormant – beneath a deciduous tree or shrub is ideal.

Helleborus
Hellebore
The hellebores are long-lived plants that gradually make more and more impressive clumps. *H. niger*, the Christmas rose, produces glistening white flowers in the very depths of winter, though it can be difficult to establish. Slightly later flowering *H. orientalis* is easier and plants often self-seed. Flowers are subtly coloured in a predominantly dusky range of purple, pink and creamy white (often the flower centres are spotted with purple). Especially desirable are the rare yellow and clear red forms.
Height and spread: 30 x 30cm (12 x 12in)
Hardiness: Hardy/Z 5–9
Cultivation: Grow in any moist but not waterlogged (preferably alkaline) soil in sun or shade.

Mahonia x media cultivars
Mahonia
Wonderfully architectural plants for the winter garden, forms of this mahonia hybrid have whorls of long, glossy, pinnate leaves, each stem crowned with upright or arching yellow flower

sprays. The most popular is the strongly upright, autumn (fall) to early winter-flowering 'Charity', but 'Winter Sun' is certainly worth seeking out, its well-formed flower heads being more frost resistant. With a little pruning after flowering, it also has a more bushy and compact habit. Others to consider include the handsomely flowered 'Lionel Fortescue' and 'Underway'. The heavy crops of blue-black berries are a boon for birds.
Height and spread: 4 x 4m (13 x 13ft)
Hardiness: Hardy/Z 8–9
Cultivation: Grow on reasonably fertile well-drained but moisture-retentive soil. Drought-tolerant in shade once established. Cut back shoot tips after flowering to promote bushiness.

Sarcococca hookeriana
Christmas or sweet box
These compact, rounded evergreens have small pointed leaves and through winter, bear tiny white blooms with a powerful fragrance, captured and concentrated in the shelter of a shady courtyard. Black fruits follow. The leaves of the hardier form *Sarcococca hookeriana* var. *digyna* are elegantly tapered and the shoot tips of the aptly named 'Purple Stem' are flushed purple, its flowers pink tinted.
Height and spread: To 1.5 x 1.5m (5 x 5ft)

Above: Viburnum tinus *'Gwenllian'*

Hardiness: Hardy/Z 6–8
Cultivation: Once established tolerates dry shade but preferably grow in moisture-retentive but well-drained, humus-rich soil and shade.

Skimmia japonica 'Rubella'
Skimmia
The skimmias make satisfying mounds of evergreen foliage with clusters of sweetly scented flowers in late winter, followed by berries on female forms. The unopened buds on the male form are deep crimson.
Height and spread: 1.2 x 1.2m (4 x 4ft)
Hardiness: Hardy/Z 7–9
Cultivation: Grow in fertile, well-drained soil in sun or light shade; most skimmias do best in slightly acid conditions.

Viburnum tinus
Laurustinus
The shrubs in this genus provide interest throughout the year. Some are grown for their flowers in winter or spring, others for their berries, some for both. The evergreen *Viburnum tinus* has white flowers in shallow domed heads in late

winter and early spring followed by bluish-black berries. 'Eve Price' is a reliable selection with pink buds and 'Gwenllian', a pretty form grown for its pink-tinged white flowers, opening from dark pink buds.
Height and spread: 3 x 3m (10 x 10ft)
Hardiness: Hardy/Z 8–10
Cultivation: Grow on any drained but moisture retentive soil including clay. Tolerates lime and partial shade.

Viburnum x bodnantense
Bodnant's viburnum
Selections of this deciduous, upright viburnum include 'Charles Lamont', 'Deben' and 'Dawn', all of which carry small, pink-shaded pompon blooms in flushes through winter, when there is a mild period. Their fragrance travels far and is a blend of honey and almond. The plants sucker mildly from the base but need little attention.
Height and spread: 2.5 x 1.5m (8 x 5ft) or more
Hardiness: Hardy/Z 7–8
Cultivation: Grow on any drained but moisture-retentive soil including clay. Tolerates lime and partial shade.

INDEX